ALSO BY BARRY FLYNN

Bernard Dunne: The Ecstasy and the Agony

John McNally: Boxing's Forgotten Hero

Legends of Irish Boxing: Stories Seldom Told

PRAISE FOR BARRY FLYNN

'Flynn knows how to tell a good story.'
—*The Evening Herald*

'This book is a must for all fight fans, young and old alike.'
—*Belfast Telegraph*

'Flynn's love for the game shines out, and few authors
could have dug deeper into boxing's archives.'
—Jack Magowan, *Belfast Telegraph*

BEST OF ENEMIES

First published in 2014 by
Liberties Press
140 Terenure Road North | Terenure | Dublin 6W
T: +353 (1) 405 5701| www.libertiespress.com | E: info@libertiespress.com

Trade enquiries to Gill & Macmillan Distribution
Hume Avenue | Park West | Dublin 12
T: +353 (1) 500 9534 | F: +353 (1) 500 9595 | E: sales@gillmacmillan.ie

Distributed in the United Kingdom by
Turnaround Publisher Services
Unit 3 | Olympia Trading Estate | Coburg Road | London N22 6TZ
T: +44 (0) 20 8829 3000 | E: orders@turnaround-uk.com

Distributed in the United States by
International Publishers Marketing
22841 Quicksilver Dr | Dulles, VA 20166
T: +1 (703) 661-1586 | F: +1 (703) 661-1547 | E: ipmmail@presswarehouse.com

ISBN: 978-1-909718-42-5
2 4 6 8 10 9 7 5 3 1

A CIP record for this title is available from the British Library.

Cover design by Liberties Press
Internal design by Liberties Press
Printed by Bell and Bain Ltd, Glasgow

Supported by

The National Lottery®
through the Arts Council of Northern Ireland

arts council of Northern Ireland

BEST OF ENEMIES

Barry Flynn

LIB
ERT
IES

NORTH

To Katrina, Meabh and Deirbhile.
And to John and to Freddie. Forever young!

CONTENTS

senior struggled to keep the unlucky fans outside the hall. Indeed, things almost got out of hand, and the police were called as Wilson handed out countless thick ears to punters who were over-eager to get in. Freddie weighed in well under the limit at almost 8st 4lb, while Keenan came in just a fraction under the weight. The talk among the spectators was all of a Gilroy victory, with some predicting – despite the fact that he and Caldwell were fighting at different weights – that a first defence against Caldwell would be a fitting gesture.

With most of Belfast praying for a Gilroy win, one person admitted that she would forgo a ringside seat and, indeed, would not be listening to the live radio coverage of the fight. Mrs May Gilroy, Freddie's mother, told Bill Rutherford in the *People*, 'I have never seen him fight and I never want to see him fight.' The rest of Belfast thought differently, and on 19 January the Lisburn Road was thronged with crowds from early lunchtime in anticipation of a piece of Gilroy magic. Having queued for over twelve hours to get the best seats in the balcony, Belfast brothers Jack and Clarke Donald were cold but undaunted in the queue outside the arena, saying, 'We wouldn't have missed the fight for the world.'

A last-minute fall-out between the camps was averted when the British Boxing Board intervened and ordered Gilroy to wear modified shorts with light stripes sewn down the sides, to avoid a clash with Keenan's colours. Gilroy's lucky black-and-red shorts had been given to him by Bosco clubmate Sean Brown prior to the start of his professional career. Regardless of the colour of the stripes on the shorts, though, Gilroy was ready for his biggest challenge.

The bill Connell put on in support of the Gilroy-Keenan fight was an attractive one. The chief supporting bout would see Caldwell face France's Simon Carnazza over ten rounds. It was appropriate that Caldwell would share the limelight on Gilroy's big night. With the bill broadcast on the BBC, Caldwell would be assured massive exposure to a British and Irish audience. His opponent had not recorded

ACKNOWLEDGEMENTS

I would wish to thank Freddie and Bernie Gilroy and the Caldwell family for their assistance in writing this book, particularly Paul and Bridie Caldwell. Teddy Gilroy's scrapbook on his brother was a true joy to behold, and I thank him for letting me access it. I would mention also John's daughters, Patricia Burns and Berna McStravick, for their recollections of their late father. Jim McCourt and Harry Enright were most helpful with their memories of the Immaculata boxing club. To Eamon McAuley, Hugh Jordan, Brian Madden, Liam McBrinn, Jimmy Donnelly and Davy Larmour, I would record my sincere thanks. I would also like to thank my father, Anthony Flynn, for his guidance. Finally, I would pay tribute to the staff of Liberties Press for their help and advice in the writing of this book.

PROLOGUE

A Solitary Man

It is a typically dark and wet Belfast Friday night in November 2005. Alone at the bar in the Fruithill bowling club in Andersonstown stands the solitary figure of John Caldwell. Gaunt and oblivious to his surroundings, John, amid the litter of spent cigarettes, ignores the bar's satellite television as some meaningless American boxing match is played out on it. Staring at his half-empty glass, the former world champion raises his eyebrows as the barman sets him up another pint of Guinness; he nods his thanks in the direction of the man who has stood him the drink. The television blares on; John Caldwell is a lonely man who has lost interest in many things in life – especially boxing.

Soon, a man in his late thirties passes by and stops with purpose. Ordering a round, the man looks up at the fight on the big screen and then at Caldwell, saying, 'My money would be on you, Johnny. My money would still be on you, wee man!' John, fighting back his irritation, lifts his head in acknowledgement and then stares back at the bar. The man pays for his round and leaves to return to his company; John now has another pint paid for in the tap. John Caldwell is ill, but the people of Belfast will never forget a legend.

The Man in the Big Picture

On a fine spring day in 1962 in Belfast's Lower North Street, Mrs Kitty Neeson from Ballymena enters Bannon's furniture shop accompanied by her ten-year-old boxing-mad son. Her young boy's hero, Freddie Gilroy, works in the shop and for fresh-faced Liam Neeson it is a dream come true. Mrs Neeson makes a polite request for Freddie to pose with her son in the street for a photograph. As usual, the boxer is happy to oblige. Neeson, dressed in short trousers and an Aran jumper, stands proudly with his hero as his mother takes the snap. Liam Neeson is as pleased as punch, having shaken the hand of an Irish boxing legend.

Forty-eight years later, in the ornate surroundings of the Belfast City Hall, the two men meet up to recreate that famous photograph. The press love the story and are out in force. Asked how he feels on being reunited with his childhood hero, Neeson responds, 'I'm still shaking.' Gilroy tells the journalists that he is delighted to recreate the photograph with the Hollywood star. 'He's the man in the big picture now,' he says. With the famous picture recreated, Freddie Gilroy returns to his humble Belfast home, while Liam Neeson returns to New York. Among Neeson's prized personal possessions is a pair of Gilroy's boxing gloves.

INTRODUCTION

Belfast is an unforgiving place. Built on the Bog Meadows, for centuries it has fought against geographical adversity to survive. Its people are survivors too. It is a friendly city, though, blessed with humour and kindness. It is also a city renowned, sadly, for fighting. All too often, the peace of the city has been shattered by unskilled and unregulated violence. However, when fighting is regulated in the form of boxing, Belfast can produce men of a class and level of skill that make them a match for anyone in the world. This is a tale of boxing in Belfast, of two men whose undoubted flair and ability put the city at the top of the sporting world for a time. That period was too short, but while the glory lasted both John Caldwell and Freddie Gilroy shone ever so brightly at the very pinnacle of an unforgiving sport.

Caldwell and Gilroy brought international greatness to Ireland and Belfast as both amateur and professional boxers. They were two exceptional exponents of the noble art who boxed their way to greatness the hard way. They were truly world-class. In an era of real legends, they were right up there with the very best. Between 1959 and 1962, both were listed consistently in the top ten of the world rankings. Boxing today is littered, perhaps, with questionable world champions and world championships – these two men were the proverbial 'real deal' in international terms.

For all the glory, this, however, is a tale laced also with tears, anguish and despair. The root cause of the unhappy side of their careers lay purely at the door of money. For every pound they earned as professionals, there were managers, trainers, seconds, hangers-on and greedy promoters all awaiting payment. Especially greedy promoters. What the two boxers were left with after deductions was a pale reflection of the solitude, sweat and tears they put into their sport. That is, sadly, the all-too-familiar story of professional boxing.

In October 1960, Gilroy was unlucky to lose to Alphonse Halimi for the European version of the world bantamweight title. After that defeat, Gilroy had been promised a rematch. Promoter Jack Solomons and Caldwell's manager, Sam Docherty, however, sensing a succession of lucrative paydays, choose to match Caldwell – then a flyweight – with Halimi. Despite the protests of the Gilroy camp, Caldwell took the crown in his first outing as a bantamweight. In the week prior to Caldwell's triumph, Gilroy had tasted disaster when he travelled to Brussels and lost a European title fight to Pierre Cossemyns. As Caldwell stood on top of the world, Gilroy's career lay in tatters. Hindsight tells us that perhaps it could have been the other way round.

In January 1962, Caldwell journeyed to Brazil to meet the legendary Éder Jofre, for the right to be named the undisputed world bantamweight champion. He was well beaten on the night and his chance of immortality was gone forever. Looking back, it could be argued that by 1962 Caldwell and Gilroy had peaked as boxers and there was nothing left for them to do, except to fight each other. That inevitable battle was a truly brutal affair; like two attack dogs sprung from their leashes, they gave each other nine rounds of hate at Belfast's King's Hall on Saturday, 20 October 1962. Gilroy won when Caldwell was forced to retire with a cut eye. That raw, spiteful fight satisfied the innate and animalistic hunger of the fifteen thousand in attendance. It most certainly satisfied – in financial terms – the joint promoters of the bout, Jack Solomons and George Cornell. The blood-fest of the King's Hall was an affront to boxing and should never have happened. In rivalry, John and Freddie's friendship was finished utterly.

A lucrative rematch proved to be too much for Freddie Gilroy. His weight problems became insurmountable. In reality, he was sick and tired of boxing. With a hefty fine issued at Solomons's behest, Gilroy left boxing in November 1963 a very bitter man. Caldwell's career limped on until 1965 when, with a damaged nose and suspect eyes, he bid goodbye to the sport. The two Belfast men had been chewed up and spat out by the sport they had loved. They had been salmon swimming in a sea infested with hungry sharks.

Retirement was not good for Caldwell and Gilroy. Both men had their demons to contend with and adjusting to normality was difficult for them. Gilroy invested his earnings in the Tivoli Bar in Donaghadee, but in 1972 the pub was to become yet another statistic in Northern Ireland's sectarian hate-fest. He moved to Australia, but four years later arrived back in Ireland looking for work. For Caldwell, life was harder. Working to make ends meet, he and his family emigrated to Canada. As he recalled, 'For six weeks, I wandered the streets looking for a job. Then I got the offer of one – clearing up sewage. That was the last straw. For the first time in my life, I felt unwanted; like a leper in a strange land. I just packed up and flew home.' As the two men hit middle age, more problems haunted them: the bottle, and relationship difficulties. The roars of Wembley Arena and the King's Hall were just ghostly memories as reality struck home. It was sad to watch.

This book is a tribute to John and Freddie. It is a reminder of the good times and the struggles they endured to carve their names indelibly into the history of Irish boxing. It is a salutary lesson too on the unforgiving world of professional boxing. John Caldwell and Freddie Gilroy were easy prey in the dog-eat-dog world of paid fighting.

For all the agony and courage they displayed throughout their careers, they were left with just pain. Others made fortunes from the blood and tears they shed on the road to the very top. Where did all the money they generated end up? Well, that's another story altogether.

I.

FROM LITTLE ACORNS

It took Mrs May Gilroy a long time to settle in Ardoyne. Hailing from the Catholic enclave of the Short Strand in east Belfast, migrating to 47 Northwick Drive on the north side of the River Lagan came as a severe jolt to her system.

The Gilroy family had established its roots in shared accommodation at 83 Seaforde Street in east Belfast. In the decade prior to Freddie Gilroy's birth on 7 March 1936, the Short Strand area had been at the epicentre of a vicious sectarian war that had coincided with the partition of Ireland. As normality returned, May and Frederick Gilroy were married in St Matthew's Catholic Church and soon three children joined them: Teddy, Freddie and Emily. Work was scarce in Belfast at the time and Freddie senior was forced to seek out a living in Manchester. Life was hard for the Gilroy family, who lived in a single room and struggled when the money Freddie senior sent home from Manchester became scarce, as it sometimes did. In 1941, the Gilroy family reached the top of the corporation's waiting list, and a house in the newly built Glenard extension of Ardoyne was considered too good an opportunity to miss.

Northwick Drive was four miles from 'home' for May Gilroy, who could not settle in to her new surroundings. For two years after the move, the Gilroy children walked daily with their mother on an eight-mile roundtrip to east Belfast to see their relatives. Not surprisingly, fitness came naturally to the Gilroy clan. Eventually the homesickness abated for May Gilroy, and young Freddie settled in at the local Holy Cross Boys' School on the Crumlin Road. It was there that the future boxing legend would learn the reality of life in Belfast. While known as a conscientious pupil, on leaving the school in 1947 he was told by his teacher Mr Higginson that he 'would amount to nothing and would be no good to anyone'. Nine years later, Mr Higginson apologised personally to Freddie before he embarked on his trip to the Olympic Games in Melbourne. It was a humble gesture by the teacher – but a bitter lesson for Freddie.

For many boys in the locality, the boxing club was an escape from their humdrum existence. Street fighting was a way of life and, at nine years of age, a button-nosed Freddie Gilroy, fed up with his inability to acquit himself in street fisticuffs, found his way to the St John Bosco boxing club in Donegall Street. It was there that his glittering career began. Father John McSparran was the inspiration behind the Bosco club. He promoted the sport as a means of keeping kids off the street during the austere war years. Situated in an attic of a grain warehouse, the Bosco was in no way salubrious. It cost two shillings to join, while the weekly dues were nine pence for working men, and four pence for schoolboys.

Trainer Jimmy McAree was a gentleman from the old school of boxing. As an amateur, he had won the Ulster senior flyweight title in 1939, representing the Red Triangle club, which had been established by the YMCA for local unemployed men. Noted for his speed and impeccable left hand, he had sparred from an early age with notable professionals such as Jim Kelly, Jackie Quinn and Peter Kane, the future world champion. Although he was destined, it seemed, for the very top as both an amateur and a professional, McAree's career was cut short when he injured an eye in a work accident. Undeterred, he became the head trainer at the Bosco club during the war and oversaw the careers of such notables as Teddy Fields, Leo McGuigan and Sean McCafferty – all of whom would emulate McAree by claiming the provincial flyweight title.

For many years, Jimmy McAree assisted clubmate Jackie McHugh in the corner of British champion Billy 'Spider' Kelly. Jimmy was devoted to boxing and to the kids of the area who entered the club. Freddie Gilroy recalled that 'he knew boxing from A to Z, and had a wonderful way of bringing out the best in you. Nobody in the gym ever feared his wrath, we just dreaded his disapproval.' McAree kept the club open five nights a week, for little or no reward. Known affectionately as the Silver Fox, McAree's grey hair was thatched with shrewdness and devotion to the sport he loved. He knew that he had unearthed a nugget in Gilroy and nurtured the precocious talent with fatherly care. 'Some kids have it, some kids don't. Freddie had it right from the start,' recalled McAree. Jimmy McAree died in 1996; his passing was a body blow to Freddie.

Gilroy was taught to box the old-fashioned way. One trick of McAree's was to place halfpennies in Freddie's closed fists when he was hitting the punch bags, and all sorts of punishments were threatened if they fell to the floor. That taught Gilroy how to punch properly, and to punch hard. Soon, Gilroy's natural talent shone through and brought him honours at the local and national levels. 'My first title came as a schoolboy when I won the club championships at the three-stone-twelve-pounds weight,' recalled Freddie. 'I then progressed on to the Down and Connor championships, which I won on four occasions, and then claimed the Ulster and Irish juvenile titles.'

By 1954, Gilroy was receiving accolades in the Belfast sporting pages as his skill came brilliantly to the fore. That year, he burst onto the national scene by beating Lisburn club's Dicky Hanna to claim the Ulster junior title, and went on to take the Irish junior title the following month by stopping Paddy Courtney of the Avona club within two minutes. 'Flyweight Freddie Gilroy is a boxer that one does not need rose-tinted glasses to watch,' wrote Left Lead in the *Irish News* after Gilroy's national victory. The Bosco boy was hot property across Ulster, in high demand by clubs eager to add his name to their annual shows. Under McAree, Gilroy learnt his trade by boxing hundreds of rounds with the then Irish senior flyweight champion, clubmate Jim Matthews. As 1955 dawned, Freddie Gilroy seemed set to plough his way with ease through the Irish senior ranks.

John Joseph Caldwell was born on 7 May 1938, in 63 Cyprus Street, a small two-up, two-down terraced house off Belfast's Falls and Grosvenor roads. Poverty and unemployment were endemic in the area, where row upon row of terraced red-bricked houses were adorned with religious icons and dominated by the twin spires of St Peter's Catholic Cathedral. John was one of six siblings born to John Caldwell senior and Bridget Browne, a native of the famous Pound Loney area of the lower Falls. The Caldwell family, like everyone else in the area, were devout Catholics, and daily Mass, devotions and prayer were the order of the day.

Bridget Caldwell was a proud housekeeper and was worshipped by her family. She was a humble but stern woman and strict with her children, who all knew the family rules by heart and the harsh consequences for breaking them. Blasphemy, swearing and impudence were all alien to the Caldwell home; praying, hard work and respect were the order of the day. On Easter Tuesday, 15 April 1941, Belfast bore the brunt of a Luftwaffe attack and almost a thousand lives were lost, as well as swathes of terraced houses in the devastated city. Temporary morgues were created to prepare the dead, and mass graves were dug in both the Milltown and City cemeteries. In Cyprus Street, John Caldwell had been blown from his cot that night as bombs landed too close by. It had been an early lesson in the need for self-defence.

John Caldwell senior worked hard to make ends meet as a joiner. One of his claims to fame was that he had built the boxing ring in the Immaculata boxing club at, of course, no charge. Like his brothers and sisters, John junior went to the nearby St Comgall's School on Divis Street, where he soon became prey to bullies. Being small in Belfast attracts the attention of street thugs. John was exceptionally petite and this was noted by local toughs eager to prove their credentials in the hard-man stakes. In the face of constant bullying, it was no surprise that the ten-year-old Caldwell joined the Immaculata club. As a boy, John ran errands for the McCusker family in Hamill Street, and when he plucked up the courage to mention to Jack McCusker that he was interested in boxing, one of the most successful partnerships in Irish boxing history began.

The Immaculata club had been founded in 1944 by the Legion of Mary in Belfast's Corn Market. The initial aim of the club had been to work with young men who had fallen foul of the law, in an attempt to provide an alternative lifestyle through sport. A year later, the club had left the centre of Belfast and relocated to Devonshire Street, in the Falls district, where it opened its doors to all of the boys in the vicinity. Since its establishment, the Immaculata had been the embodiment of boxing excellence. In the early days, trainers such as Tommy Madine, Willie Holden and the Baker brothers, Gerry and Joe, guided the youngsters through their paces. In 1946, future Olympian John McNally claimed the club's first-ever Irish boys' championship and placed the Falls Road on the Irish boxing map. He was just one of the greats who have represented the club, which has produced a long line of Ulster and Irish champions too numerous to mention.

In the 1950s and 1960s, the club went from strength to strength under the tutelage of Jack McCusker, Ned McCormick, Harry

Enright and Vinty McGurk. The Mac was a small spit-and-sawdust affair which catered to the aspiring boxers of the district. McCusker, a former middleweight champion of Ulster, was more than a mere trainer. He was a gentleman, a father figure, an unofficial social worker, and totally devoted to bettering the lives of the kids of the area. In Caldwell, he discovered a gem. Not a puncher, John boxed with skill by throwing flurries of punishing combinations which bewildered his opponents. 'I can't teach him anything. He is teaching me,' McCusker said of John's progress.

At fourteen, John left the Hardinge Street Christian Brothers' School and became an apprentice plumber with Dowling Central Merchants in Belfast's Upper Queen Street. Apart from work and boxing, religion was central to his life. Every morning, he attended Mass at St Peter's. Wednesday evenings were spent at the boys' con-fraternity in the Clonard Monastery.

With distinctive flair, John swept all in front of him, claiming the Down and Connor, Ulster and Irish boys' titles with ease. One fight, however, made the Belfast boxing fraternity sit up and realise that Caldwell was something special. That was the final of the 1954 Down and Connor juvenile championships, when he beat clubmate Seamus 'Toby' Shannon. Shannon had until then been the golden boy of Belfast boxing. In Caldwell, an opponent he had beaten pre-viously, he came up against a boxer who had become the best ring technician in Ireland – he was virtually untouchable. Caldwell pulled off a surprising win over Shannon, showing no fear as he compre-hensively out-boxed an opponent who had formerly had the Indian sign over him.

Thereafter, Caldwell blazed a trail to claim the national juvenile championship at 7st 7lb and dominate the Irish amateur scene. Religion, clean living and a devotion to training made him a skilled exponent of boxing who, by late 1955, had added the Ulster and Irish junior flyweight crowns to his burgeoning trophy cabinet (titles

Gilroy had won a year earlier, before stepping up to the senior level). In the Irish junior final on 12 December, Caldwell astounded the audience in the National Stadium with a display of combination punching to defeat army representative Chris Kelly. Still only seventeen, all was falling into place for the precocious talent that was John Caldwell. Representing Ireland at the Olympic Games in 1956 became his sole objective. He would not be denied.

2.

FREDDIE ARRIVES ON THE SCENE

In 1955, Freddie Gilroy wasted no time in making his presence felt within the senior ranks of Irish boxing. On 7 January, he was victorious in Dublin at the Munster Council's annual show when he outclassed the highly rated Des Adams of the St Andrews club. A week later, at the Ulster Hall, he was a decisive winner over Billy Haley in the annual Ulster vs. British Army bill, a victory which had the pundits sitting up and taking note of the Belfast flyweight's talent. At only seventeen, with both the Ulster and Irish junior flyweight titles to his name, Gilroy then stunned the home crowd in Dublin's National Stadium on 28 January when he outpointed the seasoned international Chris Rafter. The fight was considered an international trial and Gilroy had been the underdog. Rafter would later claim that the fact that his boxing boot had split open in the first round – which meant that he boxed two rounds in his bare feet – had hindered him, but Freddie's win ensured him a place on an Irish side to face England in London the following month.

In early February in Belfast, Freddie knocked out the Holy Family club's Dicky Connolly with a beautiful left hook to claim his first

Ulster senior flyweight crown. A week later, in the opulent surroundings of the Royal Albert Hall, Ireland lost by six bouts to four against a formidable English team. However, it was Gilroy who stole the show, with an exhibition of power punching to claim the opening victory over Gunner Derek Lloyd, a man who would go on to win the British Amateur Boxing Association (ABA) title that year.

The superb form Gilroy had shown since winning the Irish junior crown in December was interrupted, however, in Glasgow on 10 March, when he lost narrowly to the rugged Frankie Jones, a future British professional flyweight champion. That bill at the St Andrew's Hall had been between Scottish and Irish amateur select teams. For Gilroy, the defeat put his Irish championship dreams in jeopardy. He had damaged an eardrum during the fight and was advised to take a six-week break to allow the injury to heal. The result was that Chris Rafter would now have an easy route to claim the 1955 Irish flyweight title, which he duly did by defeating fellow Dubliner Des Adams on 18 March.

However, the fact that Gilroy had withdrawn from the competition left the question unresolved as to who was the best flyweight. Accordingly, Rafter and Gilroy were ordered by the board of the Irish Amateur Boxing Association (IABA) to box off for the right to represent Ireland at the international level. With places at stake against a visiting US Golden Gloves side, together with a trip to the European Championships in West Berlin, it was vital that Gilroy beat Rafter resoundingly. The bout was scheduled as part of the Arbour Hill club's tournament held at the National Stadium on 22 April.

Gilroy did all that was asked of him, pounding Rafter to the boards at the end of the first round, leaving the Dubliner unable to continue. It was a powerful display of devastating punching, which drew gasps from the audience and reinforced Gilroy's position as Ireland's top flyweight. The reward for Gilroy was, however, a snub from the IABA when they named the Dubliner as flyweight for the visit of the US Golden Gloves team in Dublin on 6 May. That tournament was a full international with a further date fixed with the Americans in Belfast on 18 May. The Belfast visit was deemed only to be a 'friendly', and Gilroy was rightly annoyed at his omission from the Dublin date. A protest was lodged by the St John Bosco club against the decision to drop Gilroy, and the newspapers – both north and south – were highly critical of the strange choice of Rafter. The Association met three days before the bill and overturned its decision.

The National Stadium was displaying the 'house full' signs on 6 May as the Americans' visit generated great interest in Dublin. Ironically, the programme for the bill reminded the crowd to consider the health of their American guests and requested that 'patrons refrain from smoking during contests two, four, six and eight' – obviously, Irish boxers were somewhat indifferent to tobacco smoke.

With the European Championships fast approaching, Gilroy entered the ring to face Tommy Reynolds, known as the Kansas Kid. Gilroy's appearance bordered on disaster. Twice in the first round, the American sent him to the canvas with vicious body shots, and the doctor was called to the Irishman's corner to check on an eye injury. As blood was streaming from Gilroy's split eyebrow, the medic had no option but to order the fight stopped. Gilroy's injury had been caused by a clash of heads. Reynolds later apologised; he was short-sighted enough to require glasses outside the ring, a condition he blamed for the clash of heads.

Although Ireland won the match by six bouts to four, it was a severe dose of reality for Gilroy, who had been made to look very average by the American. Since his eye required eight stitches, Gilroy was forced to withdraw from the Ulster Hall bill on 19 May, where Reynolds was an easy winner over Des Adams.

Despite his defeat by Reynolds, Gilroy's eye injury was by mid-May considered to have healed sufficiently for him to be chosen for the flyweight berth for Berlin. The European Amateur Boxing Championships of 1955 opened on 27 May and Ireland sent a seven-strong team. Alongside Gilroy were: the experienced Ando Reddy at bantam; Eamonn Duffy at feather; Steve Coffey, a policeman based in Manchester, at lightweight; and Harry Perry at light welterweight. Two Arbour Hill boxers, Paddy Bourke and Paddy Lyons, were selected at middleweight and light heavyweight, respectively.

Despite the high hopes of the Irish management, by the third day of competition, the team of seven had been reduced to two. Harry Perry was first to exit the championships, when he lost on points to the Italian southpaw, Gino Ravaglia. Paddy Lyons was next to bow out, when was beaten by the thirty-three-year-old veteran Július Torma of Czechoslovakia. Torma, who had won gold in the welter-weight division at the 1948 London Olympic Games, proved that he still possessed a punch as he shook Lyons with a procession of upper-cuts to claim a unanimous verdict. He would go on to claim a bronze in the division in Berlin.

Freddie Gilroy entered the ring the following morning in Berlin to box the squat, powerful Romanian Mircea Dobrescu. From Bucharest, Dobrescu had represented his country in the 1952 Helsinki Olympic Games and, in 1956, would beat John Caldwell on the way to claiming a silver medal in Melbourne. His pedigree was evident and his strength showed as he dealt easily with everything Freddie could throw at him.

In the first round, a wild swing from the Romanian as he was coming off the ropes caught Freddie flush on the jaw and sent him to the canvas for a count of eight. It was now a case of damage-limitation for the Belfast boy as he climbed to his feet to back-pedal in the face of an unrelenting attack by his opponent. The bell saved Gilroy, but it was now only a matter of time. That time duly arrived in the first minute of the second round when the Romanian nailed Freddie with a venomous right hand. Visibly shaken, Gilroy stared into the eyes of the Italian referee, who hesitated briefly before giving the order to box on. Within seconds, Gilroy was sent crumpling to the floor for the third and final time and his dream was over. At seventeen years of age, Gilroy had learned a hard lesson against a seasoned veteran; it was a dose of tough medicine.

Steve Coffey was next to bow out when he lost convincingly to Finland's Pentti Rautiainen, while Ando Reddy was on the wrong end of a poor decision in his bout with Belgium's Daniel Hellebuyck. To add to Ireland's woes, Paddy Bourke lost to the German Rolf Caroli and Eamonn Duffy was well beaten by the Polish Zdzisław Soczewiński. Ireland never got near to the medal positions. By the quarter-finals, the team was packing its bags and preparing for the flight home.

The performance of the Irish team in Berlin was extremely disappointing. In the 1953 European Championships in Warsaw, John McNally had claimed bronze and Terry Milligan had taken silver, but the class of 1955 had been made to look particularly ordinary. For the IABA, it had been a chastening exercise which had hit its coffers hard. The hype which had been created by the victory in Dublin over the Golden Gloves team in May was now a fading memory. Irish amateur boxing had been humbled in West Berlin.

The manner of the defeat to Dobrescu had caused Gilroy and McAree to reflect on what lay ahead for Freddie. It had become apparent that the Belfast teenager was maturing physically and that, in trying to remain under eight stones, he was weak in the flyweight division. The struggle against nature was now a losing battle for Gilroy and, since Ando Reddy had decided to hang up his gloves, Freddie made the natural move up to bantamweight.

A trip to Germany in June to face the cream of that country's talent saw Gilroy make his bantamweight debut in a green singlet. In front of a crowd of eight thousand in Kiel, the Irish team lost by seven bouts to three, but Freddie's win over Ernest Kappelmann was considered to have been the highlight of the evening, because of the Irishman's superb display of boxing skill. Gilroy's fine form continued in October in the National Stadium when he defeated Charles Branch of the United States in a notable 8–4 Irish victory.

Ireland's most emphatic win of the year – of the decade, in fact – came in Dublin on 25 November, with a 9–1 defeat of England's ABA champions. Chris Rafter began the rout at flyweight and was followed by Gilroy, who bested Don Weller. The fight was stopped at the start of the third round, with blood streaming from Weller's eye; Gilroy had been well ahead on points. With the Melbourne Olympic Games a year away, the bantamweight place seemed to be Gilroy's for the taking.

3.

OLYMPIC DREAMS SO HARD TO BEAT

Throughout the 1950s, Dubliner Chris Rafter may well have had nightmares about flyweights from Belfast. With Freddie Gilroy now boxing as a bantamweight, Rafter could well have thought that his path to the Olympic Games was secured. However, Gilroy's 'terrible twin' stood ready to spoil the party.

JUST HOW GOOD IS BELFAST FLYWEIGHT, JOHN CALDWELL? screamed a back-page headline in the *Irish Press* in early January 1956. That tribute had been prompted by Caldwell's emphatic victory over Roy Davis in the Ulster Hall on 4 January, in the annual Ulster vs. British Army tournament. To the roars of the Belfast crowd, John had stolen the show with a display of self-assured boxing which saw him out-point the former Welsh miner. In the programme notes that night, Caldwell said his ambitions for 1956 were 'to win the Ulster and Irish senior titles, represent Ireland in the Golden Gloves tournament in Chicago and at the Olympic Games at Melbourne'. At just seventeen, Caldwell's confidence and self-belief shone vibrantly through his boyish exterior.

Disappointment was soon to hit home for Caldwell, though. He was denied time off from work to travel to Dublin to box Rafter three days later in an official trial for the Irish international team. Rafter stopped Millisle's Ivan McCready and duly claimed the flyweight spot on the Irish team which would meet Scotland and then embark on a three-fight tour of Germany later that month.

On the same night that Caldwell beat Davis in the Ulster Hall, Freddie Gilroy brought his bantamweight bout with Jim Jones to an abrupt end in the second round when he exploded a left hook on his chin, leaving the soldier out cold, lying prone on the canvas. And on the night that Rafter beat McCready, Gilroy again proved far too good for the proverbially unlucky Des Adams. So Gilroy went to Scotland while Caldwell was overlooked.

Against Scotland, Ireland prevailed by six bouts to four. Rafter was a worthy winner against George McDade in the flyweight clash, while Gilroy had to pull out all the stops to beat Monaghan-born, Glasgow-based Dermot 'Derry' Treanor in the bantamweight bout. Both Rafter and Gilroy then acquitted themselves with integrity on the tour of Germany, each winning all three of their bouts. Gilroy's last fight against the experienced international Andreas Paffrath was eye-catching, to say the least. In a tough battle, Gilroy caught the German perfectly with his trusty left hook to end the contest rather abruptly. The *Irish Press* reported the end of the fight like this: 'a slap of leather was followed by a hollow thud as the German met the can- vas amid a very audible gasp from the three-thousand-strong patrons present'.

Rafter and Gilroy were flourishing in the ring and Caldwell knew he had work to do to get back into the reckoning, as Rafter was firmly ensconced in the box seat. Undeterred, Caldwell, as expected, kept up his impressive form by taking the Ulster senior title in early February, beating Jim McCabe of the St Georges club. Gilroy, not surprisingly, was afforded a walkover in the bantamweight division.

Ulster titles, however, hold little currency in Dublin and it was at the National Stadium that Caldwell needed to show his credentials. On 24 February, as part of the annual Corinthian club show at the Stadium, Caldwell duly captivated the Dublin crowd with a brilliant victory over the Scottish champion, Alex Woods. It was a bold statement of intent. An inspired Caldwell engrossed the crowd as he scored heavily and defended cleverly against an opponent who was vastly more experienced.

The jury was still out, though, as to who was the top dog in the flyweight division. Caldwell or Rafter? That was the question on the lips of boxing aficionados. That particular conundrum would be resolved at the Irish senior championships. The anticipation was palpable in Irish boxing circles as March approached. The fact that the winners of the respective weights in the Irish senior championships would get a trip of a lifetime to compete against the Golden Gloves champions in Chicago added extra incentive.

John Caldwell, at just seventeen, had no doubt that he was ready to take the plunge into the national senior ranks. Jack McCusker and the Immaculata club believed that they had Ireland's top talent in their possession. Only two other boxers entered the flyweight class that year: Chris Kelly, whom Caldwell had beaten in the junior final in 1955, and the champion, Rafter, who was the odds-on favourite to take the title again. Fate was to enter the equation when Rafter was forced to withdraw a week prior to the competition with a severe bout of flu. So Caldwell met Kelly in the final on St Patrick's night in Dublin. The fight was a total mismatch. Caldwell pummelled the Limerick man without mercy, forcing the referee to stop proceedings midway through the second round. It was Caldwell's speed and aggression that had won the day and gained for him a notable clean sweep of Ulster and Irish junior and senior flyweight titles.

Freddie Gilroy's progression to the senior Irish title was almost as straightforward. On 16 March, Freddie defeated – yet again – Des Adams of the St Andrews club and went on to stop Corporal Harry

Naughton in the final with a knockout. With Caldwell and Gilroy both Irish champions, it was now up to the IABA to decide if they were worthy for international duty.

Money was scarce in the Ireland of the 1950s and, after the national finals, it was announced that only two boxers would travel to Melbourne. Gilroy and Tony Byrne, who had been voted boxer of the championships, were hotly tipped. John Caldwell was classed as an outsider and, despite Caldwell's superb form, Chris Rafter was still considered Ireland's top flyweight. For Rafter, it was a case of déjà vu as, after Gilroy had been his nemesis throughout 1955, Caldwell now posed a real threat to his amateur dreams in 1956. A showdown was inevitable.

After the finals, the IABA chose three Irish select teams to box Germany in Dublin, Newry and Letterkenny. Rafter made a return to international competition in Dublin on 6 April by defeating Manfred Warme with a decisive points victory. That win ratcheted up the pressure on Caldwell. Three days later in Newry, it was his turn to put on a green vest to face Warme, whom he had beaten twice in Germany in an Irish junior select tour in September 1955. As it turned out, John put in a superb will-o'-the-wisp performance to outbox the German, scoring with ease and leaving his opponent striking out at thin air.

With this vital win under his belt, Caldwell's – and Jack McCusker's – frustration came to the fore. Speaking to the press in Newry, McCusker threw down the gauntlet to Rafter, offering him a box-off with Caldwell at the Ulster Hall on 17 April as part of the County Antrim board's final show of the season. The following day, the IABA named its team for the trip to the United States, with Gilroy secure in the bantamweight berth – and the flyweight berth notably vacant. Officials decreed that Caldwell would meet Rafter in Belfast in a showdown for the trip of a lifetime. Rafter, after requesting that the three judges appointed be from Leinster, Munster and

Ulster, agreed reluctantly to take the fight, but travelled to Belfast full of confidence.*

Since he'd been beaten just once during the 1955/56 season – by the European flyweight champion, Edgar Basel – most people thought Rafter possessed the pedigree to see off Caldwell. Still, Rafter took the fight very seriously, travelling to Belfast three days beforehand and training at the Albert Foundry club. On the evening prior to the fight, the *Belfast Telegraph*'s Jack Magowan had visited the Immaculata club and had found Caldwell looking fit and relaxed. 'I will do my best,' was all that John would say by way of prediction. Jack McCusker, knowing that Caldwell was in top shape, told Magowan, 'If Rafter wins, he'll deserve to go to America!'

Tuesday, 17 April saw the Ulster Hall jam-packed for one of the most eagerly awaited fights of Irish amateur boxing history. The cover of the County Antrim board's programme for the event was adorned with just one picture: a close-up of the local hero, John Caldwell. The Belfast crowd roared Caldwell to victory in a titanic encounter with Rafter. Speed, agility and defensive boxing all stood in Caldwell's favour, while Rafter responded with an all-action onslaught in the final round which almost swayed the judges. The

* In Letterkenny, County Donegal, in the last of the three internationals, both Caldwell and Rafter were rested by the selectors. Freddie Gilroy acquitted himself well, turning his opponent Gunter Ambras into a 'human punchbag', according to the Irish Press's Jim Magee. Gilroy had no rival in Ireland who could challenge him and his procession towards an Olympic call-up seemed straightforward. In Derry's Guildhall the following evening, though, Gilroy's powerful punch almost started a riot when he boxed an exhibition contest against local favourite Paddy Kelly. After a scrappy opening round, Gilroy caught Kelly with a left hook which sent him through the ropes and into the astounded spectators. The crowd reacted with anger and things began to turn nasty. Gilroy had opened up a hornets' nest and had to take the microphone to apologise to the packed house for his indiscretion. After a few minutes, a badly-shaken Kelly continued with the exhibition. Thankfully, the two boxers embraced at the end and were afforded a huge ovation. Fifty-eight years after the episode, Freddie laughed as he recalled the incident, 'That fellow Kelly was trying to make a name for himself in front of his home crowd, so I just put a wee bit of manners in him!'

decision was tight, but Caldwell was awarded the fight. Rafter was unhappy with the judging, but Caldwell had prevailed, proving his credentials, and was now on his way to America.

The team for the Golden Gloves tour of the United States and Canada left Ireland on 5 May 1956. It was to be a three-week trip which would see the squad compete in Chicago and Montreal and finish off with a five-day holiday in New York and Niagara Falls. The ten-member Irish team included four representatives from Ulster. Alongside Caldwell and Gilroy, Belfast's Martin Smith was chosen at featherweight, and twenty-five-year-old Royal Ulster Constabulary officer Victor Winnington at light heavyweight. In 1956, Winnington beat Paddy Lyons to become the last-ever serving policeman from the North to claim an Irish title. In doing so, he followed in a distinguished line of RUC officers to have claimed national titles. Winnington had been born in Ontario, but his parents had returned to Ireland in the 1940s and he had joined the RUC in 1952. He had represented Ireland against Germany in 1955 and possessed a powerful left hook which had seen him claim the number-one position in Ireland's light-heavyweight division.

The remaining members of the Irish team were: lightweight Tony 'Socks' Byrne, who had acquired his nickname due to his habit of pounding punchbags using socks for gloves; John Sweeney at light welterweight; Harry Perry, who was competing in his third consecutive Golden Gloves tournament, at welterweight; Eamonn McKeon at light middleweight; Peter Bourke, adding extra power to the team at middleweight; and the last boxer to be picked, heavyweight Jim Robinson, a knockout specialist who had travelled to Chicago with the Irish team in 1955. The team was accompanied by managers Christy Murphy and Garda Superintendent Paddy Carroll, president of the IABA. The team manager was to be Father McGovern of the County Down board, while Garda Officer Billy Blackwell would be the trainer in the Irishmen's corner for the duration of the tour.

On their arrival in the United States, it was fanfares and red carpets all the way for the Irish team. No expense had been spared by their American hosts, and the Irish community in Chicago provided reception after reception for them. Training was carried out under a media spotlight and heads were turned when a sparring session between Caldwell and Gilroy turned spiteful and had to be stopped by officials. Prior to leaving Ireland, the two Belfast boxers had sparred with each other in the Immaculata club, and that too had had to be called to a halt when Gilroy accused Caldwell of being far too 'eager'. It seemed that an edge had always existed between the Belfast boys. In Chicago, they both received a stern ticking off from Irish officials. In the end they shook hands, but the resentment remained.

On Friday, 11 May, the Irish team entered the Chicago Stadium, where 11,862 spectators had gathered. The *Chicago Tribune* labelled the visitors 'Ten authentic fighting Irish, ten slugging sons of Ireland'. The entertainment beforehand played up to all the Irish stereotypes, as tenors, ceilidh bands, Irish dancers, pipers – and, strangely, a Highland-fling group – performed in the arena. In fact, such was the confusion and blarney that the master of ceremonies played 'It's a Long Way to Tipperary' instead of 'The Soldier's Song', as the Irish team stood, bemused, in the ring waiting.

John Caldwell made an impressive start, outpointing the Golden Gloves champion Pete Melendez. It was a decisive and eye-opening victory for Caldwell against a seasoned champion five years his senior. Freddie Gilroy then put Ireland two bouts ahead when he proved too good for the local favourite, Don Eddington, dropping his opponent with a sweet left hook in the third round. Martin Smith looked to be in trouble in the first round of his featherweight clash when he was floored by Detroit's Harry Campbell. The Belfast fighter managed to turn the tables on his opponent, though, and by the third round he was 'belting Campbell from one end of the ring to another', according to the *Chicago Tribune*. Smith's win was followed by another emphatic performance by Tony Byrne, who beat Ken Eaton on points.

In the lead, amazingly, by four bouts to nil, the Irish team thereafter failed to live up to its excellent start. The problems started with John Sweeney being stopped by Joe Shaw in the third round of their light-welterweight bout. Harry Perry restored Ireland's four-fight cushion with an assured win over Virel Marcy, but it was downhill thereafter for Ireland as Eamonn McKeon and Peter Burke lost their bouts. In front of a home crowd at fever pitch, the Americans claimed a 5–5 draw when Victor Winnington and Jim Robinson were stopped by Ernie Terrell and Solomon McTier, respectively. The Irish contingent partied well into the Chicago night after what had been a roller coaster of a bill.

On 16 May, the Irish team travelled to Canada to face a local Golden Gloves select in front of a live TV audience and a sell-out crowd of five thousand at the Montreal Forum. The Irish team pounded its way to an impressive 7–1 victory, with Caldwell knocking Jean Claude LeClair to the canvas on four occasions, and Gilroy and Smith also impressing against their opponents. Surprisingly, Perry was beaten in his bout with Eddie Stock. As a pre-Olympic experiment, Perry had stepped up to middleweight, and found the going decidedly tougher.

To round off what had been a fantastic tour for the Irish team – and John Caldwell, in particular – the Belfast boxer was awarded the Bunny Sabbath Trophy for being the most impressive boxer on display. Nevertheless, the problem remained that the IABA had been permitted to send only two boxers to the Melbourne Games, at a cost of £600 per boxer, and it seemed that Perry, Gilroy or Byrne were the front runners.

For the Irish boxers on the American trip, the five-day break in New York and Niagara Falls, during which they dined like lords at Jack Dempsey's Restaurant on Broadway, was a dream come true. One person, though, who seemed to have over-indulged during the trip, was Freddie Gilroy. As he recalled, 'I was in New York airport and decided to weigh myself on a set of scales, which showed that I was two stones overweight, and word got back to the IABA that there was no point in picking me.' Gilroy's weight infringement would indeed affect his Olympic prospects as the summer ended.

Strong rumours soon circulated that Caldwell was to turn professional on his return to Ireland, but John was happy to scotch any talk of paid fighting. 'It's a smashing life, this amateur boxing,' he told reporters in Dublin. In Belfast, John's mother, Bridget, was emphatic that her boy would not turn professional, 'The vultures have thrown out quite a few feelers with big-money talk, but you can take it from me that John won't turn professional – not while I'm alive at any rate.'

The individual who had been behind the approaches, talking in telephone numbers and promising the world, had been the Glasgow bookmaker and promoter Sam Docherty. Living beside Caldwell in Cyprus Street was Docherty's go-between, a bookmaker's clerk by the name of Squire Maguire. Maguire had been buttering up the Caldwell family and making promises of wealth, which, to a humble lad from the Falls Road, seemed to be beyond his wildest dreams. Docherty knew exactly the extent of Caldwell's drawing power should he turn professional. More importantly, he knew exactly how much money was to be made should he secure John's signature before all the other promoters came calling.

The knock-on effect of the uncertainty caused by the interference by Docherty and Maguire soon began to manifest itself in the Immaculata club, leaving Caldwell and McCusker at loggerheads. John was an absolutely determined and ambitious boxer who had been flattered by Docherty's promises of riches and fame. McCusker was reluctant to accept that Caldwell's Olympic preparations be compromised by any talk of a professional contract. Professionals were not allowed to train in amateur clubs at the time, as paid fighting was seen as 'impure'. Eventually matters came to a head when McCusker's patience was broken by the gossip and innuendo surrounding Caldwell and he decided to lay his cards on the table. Jack reinforced the rules of the club and reminded John that no individual was bigger than the Immaculata and that *he* was in charge. Headstrong to the end, Caldwell upped sticks and left.

Attempts to resolve the stand-off failed and other Belfast clubs, not wishing to take sides in the disagreement, were reluctant to let Caldwell train in their gyms. This was a problem because he needed to be affiliated with a club to be picked for Ireland. Caldwell finally found himself a second home at the De La Salle Boxing Club, which lay adjacent to Belfast's Milltown Cemetery. The De La Salle club was linked to the local boys' home on the Falls Road and was run by former RUC Head Constable Sam Hays. Retired and living in the nationalist Ballymurphy estate, Hays was known as a referee and an able administrator in Irish boxing. He had served as the secretary of the Ulster Council and held sway in the IABA. However, within the local community, Hays was treated with suspicion. To many he was a 'peeler' first and a boxing official second. Caldwell was happy to assist Hays with the boys in the club as an interim measure, but he was still on the lookout for a better option.

By September, the IABA had been able to argue its case to the Irish Olympic Council (IOC) and, given the success of the tour of North America, it was agreed that the number of boxers to be selected for Melbourne would be increased to four. There was now a distinct possibility that both Caldwell and Gilroy would be picked on merit for the Olympics in November. Still, September 1956 was a bad month for Caldwell, even though he was the national flyweight champion. With the Irish team for Melbourne due to be announced in early October, he and Rafter remained neck-and-neck for the flyweight berth. The boxing jury was still split over who was Ireland's best flyweight. As ever, politics came into the equation, with the Dublin officials opting for Rafter, while Caldwell's supporters were vocal within the Ulster Council. Despite Caldwell's victory in the Ulster Hall in April over Rafter, the fact that the Dubliner had been laid low by flu prior to the bout had left some questions unanswered.

Fate was to play its hand when Caldwell decided that he was not fit enough to appear at the Ulster Hall on 18 September to face Rafter. The exertions in the United States and Canada in May were cited by Caldwell as the principal reasons behind his decision. However, the falling-out in the Immaculata had not helped his state of mind. If he was to box Rafter again, Caldwell was determined to be fully fit. Unfounded rumours soon circulated that Caldwell was 'running scared' and was somewhat reluctant to place on the line his position as the main contender for Melbourne.

As a replacement, the County Antrim Board, organisers of the tournament, agreed to match Rafter with the 'nut-hard' Scottish ABA champion, Peter Walsh. Such was the interest in the fight that the IABA sent three selectors to Belfast to observe Rafter's progress. It was a superbly fit Dubliner who entered the ring in the Ulster Hall to a rapturous ovation from the 1,700 spectators. He rewarded the Belfast fans with a hard-earned victory which reinforced his claim for a place on the Olympic team. As he left the arena that night, Rafter was afforded the kind of raucous support only ever given by the Ulster Hall crowd to Belfast fighters. It seemed that John Caldwell's acrimonious departure from the Immaculata had lost him supporters in his native city.

It became apparent that Caldwell and Rafter would be required to meet again to determine who should go to the Olympic Games. That battle was fixed at short notice for the National Stadium on 21 September, with the winner assured, in theory, of the trip to Melbourne. The papers made Caldwell the favourite, suggesting that the Dubliner's earlier exertions against Walsh might have left him short of stamina. Boxing fans turned out in force to see the clash. It was Rafter who took the verdict with a performance built on clever defensive boxing and counter-punching. The *Irish Press* reported that the Dublin fans 'almost took the National Stadium apart' when the decision was announced in Rafter's favour.

Caldwell's trip to the Olympic Games was in major jeopardy, as he had lost to his chief rival at the worst possible time, and in front of the selectors. It had been Rafter's greatest week as an amateur and he was now a hot favourite to be selected. The following week, Rafter must have felt assured of his place in Melbourne when the IABA chose him in the flyweight berth for the international against Wales on 5 October. Unfortunately, Rafter's hopes were shattered by the turn of events that followed.

In early October, the Irish Olympic Council (IOC) considered and endorsed a list of five boxers submitted by the IABA for inclusion in the Irish team for Melbourne. Chris Rafter had been overlooked. Harry Perry, Fred Tiedt, Martin Smith and John Caldwell were all approved, while Tony 'Socks' Byrne was added to the team provided that he could raise the necessary £600 to pay his own way. That decision by the IOC boiled down to pure economics. In Drogheda, a door-to-door collection was commenced as part of a 'Send Socks to Melbourne' campaign. That exercise saw £653 raised within two weeks to secure Byrne's place on the team. For Freddie Gilroy, who had not fought since May, it was to be heartbreak. With consistent rumours surrounding his weight and a lack of fitness, his name was not even considered.

The news that Caldwell had been chosen over Rafter was greeted by the southern-based boxing fraternity with derision. Caldwell's nomination had been endorsed by twenty-one votes to six by the IABA, and then by eight votes to four by the Olympic Council – fantastic margins considering that he had lost to Rafter less than two weeks previously. The decision was based on the belief that Caldwell was more durable than Rafter and better prepared to acquit himself over the full week of competition in Melbourne. For some, the influential presence of

Sam Hays on the IABA selection committee was seen as crucial in swaying the vote in Caldwell's favour. John Walsh, the chairman of the County Dublin Board of the IABA, labelled the decision 'the shabbiest deal in our Association's history'.

Such was Rafter's pain at being omitted from the Olympic squad that he withdrew in protest from the Irish team scheduled to box Wales in Dublin on 5 October. Caldwell stood in at short notice as Ireland hammered the Welsh by nine bouts to one. John's appearance in the National Stadium was greeted by catcalls from a Dublin crowd still incensed by Rafter's exclusion. John's fight against Roy Davies was stopped when the Welshman picked up a serious cut to his left eye, depriving Caldwell of the chance to silence the crowd with his hunger and skill. Gilroy, with a point to prove to the selectors, knocked his opponent, Peter Jones, out cold with a picture-perfect punch sixty-five seconds into the first round. It was a forceful statement by Gilroy to the watching selectors.

When the Irish team travelled to Paisley to face a tough Scottish team laced with talent on 9 October, the pressure was most definitely on John to beat the ABA champion, Peter Walsh, and silence Rafter's supporters. The BBC screened the bill live, with Harry Carpenter at ringside casting his eye over Ireland's Olympic hopefuls. He was to witness some impressive Irish performances as Scotland fell to a 7–3 defeat, with Caldwell claiming an emphatic win over Peter Walsh. It was a victory to silence Caldwell's critics. 'Here is a boy [Caldwell] who wastes no time with needless dancing. He shoots hard and sharp punches and never gets flurried. What a chance he has in Melbourne,' wrote James Sanderson in the *Northern Whig*. In the bantamweight clash, Gilroy was lucky to receive the verdict over Motherwell's Johnny Morrisey, an opponent Gilroy would defeat twice during his professional career – and whose jaw he would famously break. Harry Perry, Fred Tiedt, Tony Byrne and Martin Smith all recorded wins as Ireland claimed the Kuttner Shield with ease.

Gilroy was still reeling from having been left off the Olympic side, but he wasn't ready to give up on that dream. There was one avenue left open to him: to raise the £600 himself. He had less than a month to secure the funding but, after a superb victory in an Irish vest over the German Albert Nieswano in Banbridge on 30 October, a collection was taken among the crowd in the Adelphi Picture House. Incredibly, nearly £200 was raised for the Gilroy fund and donations soon followed from various clubs and county boards, making the total £361 by 3 November. The Irish Olympic Council met and gave the Belfast boxer a further week to make up the difference. With the six hundred workers in the Beltex factory where Gilroy worked all subscribing to the fund, the shortfall was made and, with just two days left for nominations to the Games, Gilroy was endorsed as Ireland's bantamweight representative.

For John and Freddie, securing places on the Olympic side had not been easy but, on 10 November, telegrams arrived in both Northwick Drive and Cyprus Street from the IABA, requesting sizes for team trousers, blazers, shirts and hats. The Belfast boys were on their way to Melbourne.

4.

IRELAND'S GLORY: MELBOURNE 1956

In late 1956, Ireland was an undeniably poor and depressed country. It was the social, economic, religious and political basket case of Europe. While a team of Irish hopefuls travelled to the far side of the world in search of sporting glory, for many the reality of travel was going to places such as Kilburn, Cricklewood, the Bronx or Manhattan in search of work. As the Olympic team left Irish shores, the IRA was finalising its plans for the futile Border Campaign. 'Social media' was limited to listening to the wireless with neighbours as news of the Russian invasion of Hungary and the persecution of nuns and priests stole the Irish headlines. Ireland was a conservative country but, above all else, it was poor.

In the sporting world, that year's all-Ireland hurling final had been postponed for three weeks as the country was in the grip of a polio scare. On 23 September, a packed Croke Park witnessed an epic final between Cork and Wexford, in which the Rebels won and

Christy Ring claimed his record eighth winner's medal. Meanwhile, in Gaelic football, a free-moving Galway outpointed Cork to take the Sam Maguire Cup back to the west. Manchester United's Busby Babes were champions of England, while north of the border Glasgow Rangers had retained the Scottish title. In April 1956, Rocky Marciano retired as undefeated world heavyweight champion; he was replaced in November by Floyd Patterson. Outside of sport, the most successful film released in 1956 was *The King and I*, starring Yul Brynner and Deborah Kerr. Elvis Presley was causing outrage as he gyrated his hips on *The Ed Sullivan Show*.

In mid-November, the Irish Olympic Council endorsed thirteen athletes for the Games, seven of whom were boxers. In addition to Caldwell, Gilroy, Smith, Byrne, Perry and Tiedt, Donegal man Pat Sharkey, who had emigrated from Ireland to Australia, was added at heavyweight. Gerry Martina was chosen as the country's light-heavyweight representative in wrestling. In the women's 100 and 200 metres, Kilkenny-born, Ballymena-based Maeve Kyle was selected.

Eamonn Kinsella of Donore Harriers in Dublin was picked to compete in the 110 metres hurdles. Ronnie Delany and high-jumper Brendan O' Reilly, who would go on to become famous in Ireland as a sports presenter, were training in the United States and would join the team in New York. The final piece in the jigsaw was John Somers Payne of the Cork Harbour club, who would compete in the single-handed dinghy class in sailing. The team would be managed by Christy Murphy and accompanied by Lord Killanin, president of the Olympic Council.

Problems were at hand, though. The Olympic Council reported that it was still £1,000 short of its estimated £7,500 costs, but it remained confident that the shortfall would be reached through public subscription in time for the Games. That was not to be the case. The donations dried up and a difficult decision had to be made. The unlucky competitor was to be Brendan O'Reilly, who, with his bags packed and ready at his college in Michigan, received a two-word telegram from the Olympic Council stating: 'Trip cancelled.' It was a devastating blow for the County Longford man.

On Monday, 12 November, Caldwell, Gilroy and Smith posed for photographs in Belfast's Royal Avenue with the president of the Ulster branch of the IABA, Captain T. D. Morrison, before stopping off for haircuts at the Belfast institution that was Rab Maguire's barbershop. Sporting the then-trendy crew cut, the Belfast boxers assembled in Dublin the following day and a reception was held in the Mansion House before the team boarded a bus for Shannon Airport. It was to be an unforgettable experience.

From Shannon, the team travelled to New York and, after a stop in Chicago, arrived in San Francisco. Three days of training and leisure were spent at the University of California before a United Airlines flight took them to Hawaii. Festooned with garlands, the team stayed two days on the tropical island before embarking on their final flight to Melbourne. In Australia, the weather which greeted the competitors was disappointingly poor – overcast and periodically stormy.

The Melbourne Olympic Games were the first to be held in the southern hemisphere. In all, just over 3,500 competitors from fifty-seven countries travelled to the Games. Political events cast a shadow over the Olympics, with Spain, Holland and Switzerland all withdrawing as a protest against the Soviet Union's invasion of Hungary in early November, while Egypt, Iraq and Lebanon withdrew over the ongoing Suez Canal crisis. The opening ceremony took place in the immense Melbourne Cricket Ground on 22 November. Ireland's team was afforded a rapturous reception as it entered the arena led by Tony Byrne holding the tricolour.

In the preliminary round of the featherweight division, Martin Smith was drawn against the 1952 Olympic bantamweight champion, Pentti Hämäläinen. The Finn, who had beaten Belfast's John

McNally in the Helsinki Olympic final, was vastly experienced and was a hot favourite to take gold in Melbourne. Smith had been plagued by weight problems and had spent much of his time in Melbourne in Turkish baths to make the featherweight limit. The punishment his body had endured left him weak at the weight and he was knocked to the canvas three times by the Finn on his way to a defeat on points. It was a disappointment for the team and for Smith, who had been labelled by none other than *The Ring* magazine's editor, Nat Fleischer, as Ireland's most impressive boxer of the US tour in May that year. Hämäläinen would go on to claim a bronze medal in Melbourne when he lost in the semi-final to Great Britain's Tom Nicholls. Martin Smith died in Seattle on 25 November 2012, fifty-six years almost to the day after his one and only appearance in an Olympic boxing ring.

In the heavyweight clash between Pat Sharkey and Sweden's Thorner Ahsman, the Donegal man walked into a clean right hand in the third round, and his Olympic dreams were at an end. The omens looked bad for the Irish boxers, but that was not all. In the aftermath of his defeat, Sharkey was ordered by Irish officials to vacate his room in the Olympic village, thus saving a paltry fee of £3 and 10 shillings (Australian) per day. The request was not well received by the rest of the team, but Sharkey agreed to leave the village and took up residence – at his own expense – in a cheap hotel in Melbourne so that he could watch his teammates.

That tiff was merely the tip of the iceberg when it came to the miserly attitude of the Irish Olympic officials. A further row broke out when it was discovered that the Irish team were to have their daily allowance cut from 14 shillings to 5 shillings, an amount that would barely have bought a cup of coffee and a sandwich. The *Melbourne Globe* reported that 'Ireland's boxers are a wild bunch. And because of the raw deal they're getting in expenses, they've every reason to be wild'. The expenses issue made Ireland the laughing stock of the

Olympic village. Eventually, a deal was brokered which saw the officials relent and agree to provide 10 shillings per day to each team member. The damage had been done, though, and the embarrassing episode created bad feeling between Ireland's competitors and their officials.

Both Caldwell and Gilroy made their debuts in the boxing tournament on 26 November. In the opening round of the flyweight competition, Caldwell had been afforded a bye. His first opponent, Yai Shwe of Burma, fell victim to Caldwell's unique style of working inside with quick punches and then switching his attacks from body to head. The *Irish Independent* reported that Caldwell had been labelled the 'Sinister Leprechaun' by the press, such was his style of fighting. With menacing precision, John caught his opponent's chin in the second round, forcing him to take a mandatory count. In the third, such was the barrage of punches thrown by Caldwell that the referee was forced to intervene to stop the punishment, with Yai Shwe trapped on the ropes. John's victory was greeted with glee on the streets of the Falls Road in west Belfast. The news of the win broke on Raidió Éireann and, immediately, hordes of journalists rushed to Cyprus Street, where they clambered for a quote from John's mother, Bridget. 'I knew all the time that John could do wonders in Melbourne,' she said. 'Ever since he left I've been terribly anxious. I'm praying now that he gets to the final.'

Gilroy's opponent in his opening bout in the bantamweight division was the Russian Boris Stepanov, who was representing the Soviet Union. As European champion, Stepanov was an overwhelming favourite to see off Gilroy, who was a considered to be a complete novice in comparison. The Soviet Union's invasion of Hungary had created antagonism that would manifest itself throughout the Games, as the communist and capitalist countries strove for supremacy. That bitterness was played out particularly in the boxing ring. After a cagey opening two rounds, Gilroy made world headlines when he knocked the Russian out cold with a sweet left hook. 'I remember there was a lot of tension in the air over the Hungary invasion and my fight with the Russian was seen as a clash of East and West,' Gilroy recalled in 2005. 'He was the hot favourite, but I caught him with a perfect left hook and he went down and was not getting up. The crowd were going absolutely wild as this was one in the eye for the Russians.'

A. P. MacWeeney's introduction to his *Irish Press* article on Gilroy's victory was colourful and truly memorable:

> Boy, oh, boy! You should have heard the rafters ring at the West Melbourne Stadium tonight when Freddie Gilroy, the boy who was only added to the Irish team as an afterthought, scored a third-round knockout over Soviet Russia's midget tank and European bantamweight champion, Boris Stepanov. The crowd rose to their feet as one man, and the cheering and clapping continued for several minutes as Gilroy danced around the ring for joy while Stepanov's seconds worked over the Russian who lay slumped, semi-conscious, in his corner.

Afterwards, the Irishman's dressing room was swarmed with journalists and well-wishers who all wanted to meet the man who had caused the greatest upset of the Games so far. 'I never dreamed I would knock him out,' an excited Gilroy told the media, 'I just boxed to the instructions of my corner and coming into the third round, I felt that I might just pull it off.' On the punch, he added, 'It was a beauty. When he missed me with a hook, I just saw an opening and let fly.' When asked why he was sporting a red nose after the fight, Freddie replied, 'Sure that's only sunburn I got at the opening ceremony on Thursday.'

Fred Tiedt, in his opening bout, beat on points the fancied Pole Tadeusz Walasek – who would go on to win silver and bronze medals at the two succeeding Games. The Dubliner was then drawn to meet the American representative Pearce Lane in the quarter-final. Lane was the reigning US Army and Services champion and was considered a tough adversary. However, it was Tiedt who made all the running in the fight and he was not troubled by Lane throughout the three rounds. Tiedt's cat-like footwork and ability to find his punches from range saw him home on a unanimous decision. Ireland had claimed its first medal of the Games – a bronze. However, Harry Perry, who had been afforded a bye in the opening round of the light-welterweight division, in his first bout lost on points to the French representative, Claude Saluden.

The draw for John Caldwell for his quarter-final saw him matched against the Australian Warner Batchelor. One fight away from a medal, the Belfast boxer had to face a classy fighter as well as a partisan home crowd in the packed arena. For nine minutes, Caldwell boxed assuredly. He broke through his opponent's defence early on in the bout to score heavily. The third round saw Batchelor happy to mix it up at close quarters with Caldwell, who had already built up a credible lead. Bobbing and weaving, feinting and boxing cleverly on the defence, Caldwell was a clear winner and assured himself of at least a bronze medal when his hand was lifted in victory.

Freddie Gilroy knew that the luck of the Irish was most definitely with the boxers as he entered the ring to face the tough, beetle-browed Italian Mario Sitri in the quarter-final. Gilroy was in control as his opponent rushed at him with abandon, picking up three cautions for indiscretions with his head and gloves. In the second round, the Italian was caught by a clean punch which shook him badly and caught the collective eyes of the judges. Thereafter, Freddie turned on the style, catching Sitri with a series of short hooks which were greeted with a chorus of 'Oh! Oh! Oh!' as each punch landed. In the end, Gilroy was an easy winner and Ireland and Belfast rejoiced as a third bronze medal was assured within an hour.

Remarkably, the run of luck got even better. In the lightweight class, Drogheda's Tony Byrne was victorious. In his opening clash with Josef Chovanec, Byrne received a stroke of luck when the referee disqualified the Czech boxer. On receiving his second warning for holding, Chovanec charged at Byrne with his head aimed at the Drogheda man's chest, leaving the referee no option but to disqualify him. He went on to win his quarter-final match in a tough battle against the fancied US marine Louis Molina.

With four boxers now through to the semi-finals, Ireland was on the verge of boxing history. The press again clamoured at the doors of Mrs Gilroy and Mrs Caldwell in search of quotes. The *Irish Independent* ran a special article on the Belfast boxers and, in Cyprus Street, the Caldwells' pet budgerigar, Sparky, stole the show with his display of talking skills in honour of John. The bird was adept at saying the word 'champ' on the mention of John's name.

The day of the semi-finals duly arrived, with Caldwell first into the ring to face the fiery little Romanian Mircea Dobrescu, the same Romanian who had stopped Gilroy in two rounds at the 1955 European Championships. John seemed to lack any of the sharpness which had seen him to victory in his earlier contests. Despite winning the first round, he tired and was punished in the two remaining rounds. Yet the decision was still too close to call as the fight went to the judges. A split decision was the verdict. With two judges opting for Caldwell and two for the Romanian, it fell to the Polish judge to cast his deciding vote in favour of Dobrescu; Caldwell's Olympic Games were at an end. Dobrescu would go on to miss out on a gold medal to Great Britain's Terry Spinks. Distraught and in tears, Caldwell left the ring to be consoled by the Irish team.

As Caldwell returned to the dressing rooms, Freddie Gilroy was preparing to meet his own destiny in the shape of Germany's Wolfgang Behrendt, who was the main hope for a gold medal for a unified German team. The Australian crowd had taken Gilroy to their hearts and cheered wildly as the bell rang to signal the start of the fight. In whirlwind fashion, Gilroy set about his task with gusto, catching Behrendt with classy hooks and shaking him solidly with a vicious right hand. The German, though, began to show his boxing craft, using the ropes to get out of trouble and scoring on the counter-attack. With one round left, the fight was very much in the balance. Gilroy's barrage was relentless and he seemed to be on top as the final bell rang, to wild applause.

Ireland, it seemed, had secured itself a place in the bantamweight final. It was now in the hands of the judges. Like the bombshell which had hit Caldwell a mere half an hour earlier, though, the news was not good. Again, the five judges were split evenly and it fell to the Russian judge, who cast his decisive vote in favour of the German. The decision was greeted with derision within the crowded arena. There was, however, nothing that could be done. It was a body blow to Gilroy and the Irish team. Two bronze medals had been assured, but two semi-finals had been lost by the closest of margins.

It was a saddened John Caldwell who consoled a tearful Freddie Gilroy on his return to the dressing rooms. The dreams of the two Belfast boys were over. Back home, though, Belfast rejoiced at their achievements.

Tony 'Socks' Byrne's opponent in the lightweight semi-final was to be the German, Harry Kurschat. Expectations were high for the Drogheda man. It was not to be, however, as the German displayed greater technique and scoring ability to gain the decision over Byrne on points. It was bronze again for Ireland.

Fred Tiedt then stepped through the ropes to face the Australian Kevin Hogarth in front of a partisan home crowd for the right to qualify for the welterweight final. Tiedt put on an exemplary display as he kept out of the Australian's reach for the duration of the fight. He adopted a defensive mode and baffled Hogarth by bobbing and weaving on the ropes, then launching his own blistering attacks on the counter. A carpenter by trade, Tiedt displayed excellent boxing artistry as he waltzed into the final – assuring himself of at least a silver medal – where he would meet the Romanian Nicolae Linca. Tiedt was now the country's sole representative in the Olympic finals. In his semi-final, Linca had beaten the fancied Commonwealth champion Nick Gargano. The press had considered the Romanian as fortunate to come through that bout, a fact that made Tiedt the favourite going into the final. Alas, history records that Tiedt was beaten on a split decision.

It was a result that was very hotly disputed. When the match was awarded to Linca, the decision was met with boos and slow hand-claps. The anomaly was that Tiedt had been awarded more points in total than the Romanian, but was denied on a majority verdict. A Romanian referee was heard to say to Irish Olympic Council President Lord Killanin that Linca had been well beaten. It was said that Killanin had been asked by an official to make his way to the ring to present the Irishman with the gold medal in the belief that the result had gone in Tiedt's favour. Wisely, Killanin retained his seat, not wishing to tempt fate. Tiedt was later to recall that, after the fight, he had tried to lodge an official complaint but was told by officials that he was required to pay £5 for it to be heard. Neither he, of course, nor any of the Irish officials, had £5 to spare – so the result stood.

In the official report on the 1956 Games produced by the International Olympic Committee, the fight between Tiedt and Linca was mentioned specifically:

Welterweight: Probably the most unlucky boxer was Tiedt (Ireland) who lost a close final to Linca (Romania) after he had come through three very hard fights in his division against Walasek (Poland), Lane (USA) and Hogarth (Australia).

Ireland's participation in the Olympic Games ended gloriously on Saturday, 1 December, when Ronnie Delany burst through the field to take the gold medal in the 1,500 metres final. The Arklow-born twenty-one-year-old ran the race of his life to beat Germany's Klaus Richtzenhain and local favourite John Landy, claiming Ireland's first-ever track gold medal. In front of 120,000 fanatical fans, including all of the Irish team, Delany conjured up every last ounce of determination to cross the line in front of the field. Having broken the Olympic record, he sank to his knees from sheer exhaustion to say a prayer of thanks. In Dublin, milkmen and postmen all shouted the news of the epic victory throughout the darkened streets of the early morning.

Delany's gold was the ultimate triumph, crowning a fantastic two weeks for Irish sport. The celebrations were long and joyous, and Ireland's reception at the closing ceremony was rapturous. Looking back in 2007, Caldwell recalled with pride those weeks in 1956:

> We were away from home for six weeks and it was a magnificent experience for all of us. We stopped off in New York, San Francisco and then Hawaii – places which we had only seen in the films. I was the baby of the team and Maeve Kyle looked after me in particular. I will never forget the immense pride I felt walking behind the flag at the opening ceremony. As it turned out, it was the most successful set of Irish boxers ever to go to an Olympic Games as, apart from my medal, we won two bronze and one silver medal via Freddie Gilroy, Tony Byrne and Freddie Tiedt. But, for me personally, it was such an honour to be picked in the first place and I was so overjoyed to be representing Ireland and wearing the green vest on such a stage. Just being there at such a young age was something really special and I still find it hard to explain the feeling.

For some of the Irish team, the excitement of the return home from Melbourne was dampened by the news that there had been a hiccup in the travel arrangements. The result was that Ronnie Delany, Harry Perry and Tony Byrne all volunteered to remain behind in Australia and wait for a later flight. For the three athletes, it was an eventful return, as engine trouble in Hawaii meant that they were put up in the Waikiki Beach Hotel in Honolulu for four days as alternative arrangements were made. The only other member of the Irish team who remained in Australia was manager Christy Murphy, who had contracted pneumonia and was hospitalised; he had missed all the glory through illness.

The Irish team – minus Delany, Perry and Byrne – arrived home on a flight from New York that landed at Shannon Airport at 9.15 on the morning of Tuesday, 11 December. The mayor of Limerick, Alderman Ted Russell, welcomed the team one by one as they left the plane to prolonged cheering. Martin Smith was first off, followed by Maeve Kyle, and then a smiling Gilroy was greeted with prolonged applause and a barrage of flashbulbs as he produced his medal. Wrestler Gerry Martina appeared next, alongside a sunburnt Fred Tiedt, who was greeted with a hug by his father. They were followed by Caldwell, still sporting two bruised eyes from his exploits against Mircea Dobrescu. Alderman Russell addressed the team, telling them that Ireland was 'proud of the distinctions you have brought to our country.'

The Shannon Airport welcome was merely the start of a day of celebrations, as the team travelled across the midlands to Dublin. The first stop for the heroes was in Nenagh, County Tipperary, where they were welcomed by the local Christian Brothers' Boys' Band. The streets were thronged with well-wishers, and a civic reception was held in the team's honour. Gifts and mementos were given to the athletes and boxers and, after a rendition of the national anthem in the pouring rain, the team was cheered back onto their bus. After Nenagh it was Portlaoise, where it was fair day, and thousands of farmers and townspeople applauded and fought to shake the hands of Ireland's newest heroes. In the Airds Hotel, another reception was held where the great and the good of County Laois paid warm tribute.

In the early evening, the highlight of the homecoming ceremonies took place in the Mansion House in Dublin, where the Lord
Mayor, Robert Briscoe, TD, was master of ceremonies. Word soon
broke on the streets of Dublin that the team had arrived, and thousands waited patiently in Dawson Street to glimpse the sporting
stars. Fred Tiedt, as the hometown hero, was mobbed by well-wishers. Amid flashbulbs, cheers, applause and handshakes, Ireland's
sporting heroes, who had left the island on a wing and a prayer, had
returned to a country thrilled by their collective performance.

On their arrival back at Belfast's Great Victoria Street station,
massed crowds cheered and brandished rattles to greet Caldwell,
Gilroy and Smith. All three were carried shoulder-high through the
terminus and into the cold Belfast night air. The Lord Mayor of
Belfast, Alderman Harcourt, contacted the families of the boxers to
pass on congratulations on behalf of the city, and promised that a
civic reception would be held in their honour. As Caldwell recalled:

> The whole of Cyprus Street and most of the Falls Road was out to
> cheer me on my return to Belfast. When I recall the feeling inside me
> and I think of standing there on that podium in Melbourne with my
> medal it just makes me so proud. It was a dream come true and some-
> times I have to pinch myself and question whether it really happened.

At the Beltex factory in Flax Street, Gilroy was afforded an ecstatic
welcome by his work colleagues as he was paraded on the back of an
open lorry festooned with boxing ropes. Mrs Magee, the manager of
the canteen, presented the medallist with an electric shaver as a
token of appreciation on behalf of the employees.

John and Freddie were soon deluged with invitations from all
over Belfast and beyond to official dinners, guest appearances and
visits to local boxing clubs. They were heroes and they soon learned
that life after the Olympic Games would not be the same. Caldwell,

Gilroy and Smith received their civic reception in the Ulster Hall on 19 December. The Lord Mayor made a presentation in the ring to each boxer, as a token of the city's appreciation. The occasion coincided with the annual Ulster vs. British Army Select match, but the locals were left disappointed when the army side triumphed by nine bouts to one. Gilroy was Ulster's only winner and the only one of the three Olympians to box. He outpointed Sapper Alex Ambrose with a cool and assured performance. It was to be his last appearance as an amateur boxer before his loyal home crowd.

Ireland's achievements in the 1956 Olympic Games were remarkable to say the least. Of twelve competitors, five took home medals. Add to that the fact that Belfast's Thelma Hopkins had taken a silver medal for Great Britain in the women's high jump, and it was a fantastic return for the island in world terms. Throughout the rest of December, Irish cinemas were packed with crowds who cheered wildly as they relived the heroics of the team on newsreels. It had been a magical Olympic Games for Ireland, but as 1957 approached, both John and Freddie had some serious thinking to do about their futures in the ring.

5.

FREDDIE GILROY:
THE CHERUB WITH THE CLOUT

With the memory of his Olympic exploits only weeks old, Freddie Gilroy took the plunge into the paid ranks. In Belfast boxing terms, he was the biggest addition to the professional scene since John 'Rinty' Monaghan retired as world flyweight champion in 1950. Speaking exclusively to the *Irish Press* in early January 1957, the twenty-year-old explained, 'Pro boxing here I come. Yes, I have fought for the last time as an amateur. From now on, I work for figures – not fun. There will be no turning back. I have applied for my professional licence and will make my debut next month.'

Gilroy felt that he had peaked as an amateur and it was now natural for him to go professional. As for a manager, there really was only one choice – Jimmy McAree. 'Jimmy is like a brother to me and knows me better than I know myself – what he doesn't know about boxing isn't worth knowing,' said Gilroy. 'One day, Jimmy believes that I will fight for a British title. I do hope he is right.' It was a prediction which was to prove to be something of an understatement.

In the *Irish Press* interview, Gilroy paid tribute to his mother and father, who he said had given their blessing to his decision to turn professional. Despite the promises of a lucrative boxing career, he said he was keeping his £6-a-week job as a cloth examiner at the Beltex factory in Ardoyne's Flax Street. He was a man who possessed a low boredom threshold, and the prospect of idleness during the day was not on his agenda.

Gilroy's professional career was eagerly anticipated by the Belfast public. He was pure box-office material. He was clever and exciting and, most importantly, he possessed a punch, or, as people in Belfast would put it, he could 'dig'. He was precisely the shot in the arm which Irish professional boxing needed at a time when the sport was receiving criticism from on high.

A serious riot which had occurred in the King's Hall in the aftermath of Billy 'Spider' Kelly's controversial defeat to Charlie Hill in January 1956 had sent shockwaves through the sport. That night Kelly, Derry's favourite son, had brought a massive crowd to the arena to see him defend his British title. Trouble began after London referee Tommy Little gave the decision to Hill, a tough Scot, in front of twelve thousand bemused spectators. Initially, all was calm, but then chants and boos rose to a crescendo. Eventually, beer bottles exploded with froth as they bounced into the ring, followed by the first of a barrage of wooden chairs.

The great and the good – including the Lord Mayor of Belfast – were hit by flying missiles as the rioting intensified. The master of ceremonies, James Allen, was felled in the ring when a chair hit him full on as he attempted to restore calm by leading a rendition of 'When Irish Eyes Are Smiling'. Undeterred, Allen brushed himself off and made a second attempt at the song, only to suffer the same fate, as another chair caught him from behind. Order was eventually restored only after a series of baton charges within the Hall by the Royal Ulster Constabulary. However, the King's Hall was left in a mess, and boxing had again been dragged through the gutter. The pressure was on the authorities to act.

In August 1956, Belfast City Council voted narrowly not to ban boxing from its ornate Ulster Hall. Boxing within the opulent surrounding of that arena, where legendary heavyweight champion John L. Sullivan had provided a boxing exhibition in 1887, had always had its critics, who felt that the sport was not a suitable attraction. Boxing in the 1950s took place twice weekly in the hall with queues forming outside on Wednesday and Saturday nights in anticipation of a night's cheap entertainment.

Boxing was synonymous with the Ulster Hall and it was there that Gilroy's climb through the rankings would commence. Immediately, the pundits predicted that Gilroy would mow his way through the bantamweight division and claim the British title with ease. His debut was scheduled for Saturday, 9 February. The man chosen as the sacrificial lamb for the occasion was Derek McReynolds, from Old Colwyn in north Wales, who, in only his fourth professional bout, had yet to record a victory.

Promoter George Connell knew that he was on to a winner. With admission prices ranging from 3 shillings to 5 shillings, Gilroy's debut was exceptional value, and the fans flocked to Bedford Street in eager anticipation of a winning debut. The two-thousand-capacity Ulster Hall had the 'house full' signs displayed an hour before the bill began. When Gilroy entered the ring at half past nine, the crowd, which overflowed into the corridors, cheered their homecoming hero to the rafters. The expectation was for a spectacular start to an eagerly anticipated career. The crowd would not be disappointed.

It was almost unfair on McReynolds, as Gilroy attacked and fired his power-laden left hook to the head and body. Twice the Welsh boxer was hammered to the canvas in the first round, only to face further onslaughts as Gilroy pounced from his corner after counts of eight. With Jimmy McAree urging his protégé to take his time, Gilroy showed indifference and went all-out for the kill. A helpless McReynolds rolled around the ropes as excited roars resounded around the perfect acoustics of the arena. Gilroy caught McReynolds square on the jaw with a ferocious left; the time had come and McReynolds folded like a defective deckchair. Referee Jim McCreanor shouted 'out', and the crowd rose as one. Eventually, McReynolds made his way gingerly to his feet. It was job done for Gilroy, who pocketed a measly £5 for his night's work. It had, though, been a mere two minutes of farce to break him into the professional ranks.

Two weeks later, at the same venue, a capacity crowd settled down to watch Gilroy take on and dispatch Dundee's Danny McNamee in two minutes and forty seconds of the second round. McNamee had been a late substitute for Rudy Edwards and had arrived in Belfast by plane merely forty minutes before his fight with Gilroy. The announcement that Edwards had withdrawn was met with howls and foot-stomping. There was now a real threat of disorder. Thankfully, McNamee arrived just in time to fill the vacancy and was met immediately with a flurry of fists from Gilroy.

For McNamee, Dundee must have seemed a million miles away but, remarkably, the substitute did enough to survive the first round and was warmly applauded by the crowd as he bobbed and weaved his way to safety. In the second round, the cherub-faced Irishman connected with a clean punch which flipped his game opponent onto the flat of his back. Seconds after the unmistakeable sound of McNamee's body bouncing on the canvas, he was counted out – to rapturous applause in the Hall. Two weeks, two fights, two knock-outs and two crisp five-pound notes was the tale of Freddie's paid career by 23 February 1957.

On the eve of St Patrick's Day, Gilroy, the newly christened Baby-Faced Assassin made his debut in the cavernous King's Hall in south Belfast in front of an estimated crowd of twelve thousand. Topping that bill was Derry's former British and Empire champion Billy Kelly, who would take on Boswell St Louis of Trinidad and Tobago. Such was Kelly's drawing power that buses of his supporters began arriving in the early morning from Derry. The doors at the arena opened at 4.30 PM, and multitudes of quite 'refreshed' fans began packing the balcony for the best view of the proceedings.

Gilroy's original opponent, Rudy Edwards, threw yet another spanner into the works when he again withdrew – this time a day before the bout, with flu. For promoter George Connell, another headache ensued in an attempt to match Gilroy and keep the fans satisfied. The stand-in was to be Manchester's Jackie Tiller, a thoroughbred of a journeyman, who had lost twelve of his seventeen paid fights, and who should never have been matched against Belfast's newest wonder boy.

Gilroy took his time and dished out a boxing lesson to the Mancunian in a fight which went the allotted six rounds. In the fifth, Gilroy unleashed a left cross which sent Tiller to the canvas for a count of eight. He hung on bravely, though, in the face of one-way traffic to see out the contest and taste defeat. Gilroy received £20 for his controlled exploits in the King's Hall that night; Billy Kelly lost to Boswell St Louis. As the career of the Derry legend was waning, the King's Hall witnessed the waxing of a new Irish star.

On 30 March, Gilroy returned to the Ulster Hall and thrilled the capacity crowd as he disposed in two rounds of Glasgow's Jim Cresswell. It was Gilroy's fourth outing in less than two months, and he reinforced his reputation with a clean knockout. 'It was the most perfect punch you could imagine,' wrote Left Lead in the *Irish News* on the following Monday. 'This, my friends, is it,' added the correspondent. 'We have a puncher, not a fighter, who methodically pounds an opponent to submission. He is the most destructive puncher, pound for pound, that I have ever seen.' This was an incredible accolade for Gilroy from one of the most respected boxing pundits in the sport.

On Gilroy's telling punch, Left Lead elaborated: 'It was as sudden as a cobra striking. The tightly curled brown glove thundered flush into the jaw of Cresswell as he came off the ropes. For a split second he swayed, then collapsed in a half roll as if his body was hinged.' Cresswell ended up in Belfast's Royal Victoria Hospital with concussion that evening, but Belfast had a new hero. 'I hate slappers,' said manager Jimmy McAree to the press, as he showed them Gilroy's bruised knuckles. Indeed, so tightly had Freddie's hands been gripped within his gloves that he was unable to sign autographs for a full ten minutes after the fight. As the masses exited the Ulster Hall, the talk was about Gilroy, the 'killer' bantamweight.

The chattering classes of boxing were taking note. The British bantamweight champion, Scotland's Peter Keenan, whose father hailed from Dungannon, County Tyrone, had retained the title in 1954 when he defeated George O'Neill at the King's Hall. Keenan, at twenty-eight years of age, was looking very anxiously over his shoulder as the Gilroy roller coaster gained momentum. A clash between the champion and the pretender to the throne looked inevitable.

Gilroy had time on his side and a date to keep with Liverpool's crafty Terry McHale in the Ulster Hall on 13 April. McHale was duly swept aside by the talented southpaw when, at the start of the second round, he took a left hook to the chin which was described in the *Belfast Telegraph* as being 'as sweet as marzipan'. Working at speed, Gilroy had stalked McHale until he felt that the time had arrived. In a split second, a left hook to McHale's ribs was followed up with the same punch to the jaw and it was a case of 'goodnight Terry'.

For promoter George Connell, the good times were reflected through massive takings at the door of the Ulster Hall, yet Gilroy received merely £20 for his appearance. On the downside for Connell, Belfast City Council had opted to close the Ulster Hall for redecorating from mid-April to June 1957. Gilroy was going to be forced to display his unquestionable talent elsewhere as his climb up the British rankings continued. The problem was that not too many boxers were willing to face the man with the most talked-about punch in British boxing. Opponents were proving difficult to attract.

A crowd of thirty thousand paid in to Glasgow's Firhill Park for the bill in which Gilroy's next outing took place, on 22 May. Boxing on the undercard of the Sam Docherty-promoted bill, the Clouting Cherub, as Gilroy was now nicknamed, was playing second fiddle to Peter Keenan, who was to defend his British and Empire title against fellow Scot John Smillie. With Keenan's chance to make history by claiming his second Lonsdale Belt outright, the bill had captured the imagination of the Glasgow public. Gilroy's opponent was the Scottish Archie Downie, who, in only his fifth fight, was ripe for the taking.

As the massive crowd sat chilled to the marrow in the open air of Partick Thistle's football ground, Keenan stepped up to the plate just after nine in the evening and stopped Smillie in six rounds. With his second Lonsdale Belt secured, Keenan – and most of the crowd – drifted off, and Gilroy's entry into the ring at 10.28 PM was witnessed by relatively few. By 10.36, Gilroy was leaving the ring; Downie had succumbed to the Belfast boy's feared left hook in the second round. In the *Belfast Telegraph*, Jack Magowan described the Scot's demise: 'like a yacht keeling over in a squall; the count was unnecessary'.

'You can only beat what is put in front of you' is an old adage in sport. However, what was being put in front of Freddie Gilroy was less than testing. For an amateur who had almost claimed the top prize at the Olympic level at the age of twenty, it was not surprising, given the less-than-inspiring choice of opponents, that he had begun his paid career in whirlwind fashion. However, patience was required in the managing of Gilroy's career. Belfast's boxing history at that time contained an emphatic lesson in how not to handle the professional career of an Olympic medallist. That was John McNally.

McNally had made history at Helsinki in 1952 when he had claimed Ireland's first-ever boxing medal by taking silver in the bantamweight class. He was a star in his own city and took the plunge into the professional ranks in 1954 for a paltry £40 signing-on fee with joint managers Sam Docherty and Jimmy Callaghan. Although McNally won his first six fights, things soon started to go wrong. A defeat to Joe Quinn in March 1955 at the King's Hall was the start of McNally's demise as a paid fighter. In essence, there was no plan, no support and, most emphatically, no money. McNally had appeared on the same bill as Gilroy in Glasgow on 22 May, where he had been knocked out in seven rounds by Guy Gracia. At the age of twenty-five, Ireland's brightest young hope of 1952 had, within the space of five years, ended up a mere journeyman.

Jimmy McAree was never going to let Freddie Gilroy travel the same route as McNally. Speaking in the *Weekly News*, McAree was critical of those who had questioned the abilities of the opponents Gilroy had met. 'Freddie will stay in the novice class as long as I can keep him there,' said McAree. 'More good young boxers have been spoiled by being tried too highly too quickly, and I'm not letting it happen here.' In the medium term, the British title was the primary aim for Gilroy. It was just a matter of a time and a place for that to occur – and that depended on Peter Keenan.

The champion knew deep down that his career was coming to an end, and Gilroy was now the man in the frame. The one question hanging over Gilroy's career was his ability to last eight, ten or even fifteen rounds. As an amateur, he had been confined to three rounds and, in his paid career, he had never been beyond six. Stamina was the key to success in the professional game, and Gilroy's had yet to be tested.

Within a month of his first outing in Glasgow, Gilroy was back at Firhill Park for another Sam Docherty promotion. Topping the bill on Tuesday, 26 June was supposed to be a clash between Charlie Hill and Belfast's Jimmy Brown for Hill's British featherweight title. Add to that an international contest between Peter Keenan and the highly rated Canadian champion Pat Supple, and Docherty was on to a winner, with the prospect of another thirty thousand attendance. With a notable lack of British bantamweights willing to box Gilroy, Docherty secured the services of Andre Gasperini, a Frenchman who had been rated number four in the European flyweight ranks.

Docherty's plans were scuppered, though, when first Hill and then Supple withdrew for personal reasons. The weather forecast predicted rain for Glasgow for the night of the bill. With a lack of quality fights – and, more importantly, cover from the elements – Docherty began to panic. In his programme notes, the Glasgow promoter talked about his 'week of worry, a gigantic telephone bill and many headaches'. However, Docherty's work paid off and Keenan was matched with France's Robert Tatari while, for Jimmy Brown, the Parisian Mostique Meslen agreed at short notice to make up the numbers. The bill was saved and the public began buying tickets with gusto.

Boxing News that week had placed Gilroy as number seven in the British bantamweight division, with Belfast's Jimmy Carson considered as the main contender to Keenan's crown. Carson's elevation to prime challenger had been due to his surprise defeat of world champion Alphonse Halimi in a non-title fight at the Harringay Arena in early June 1957. Given that result, Carson had eclipsed Gilroy as Belfast's main bantamweight hope and was the man Gilroy had to beat to claim a crack at Keenan. Prior to Carson's fight with Halimi, boxing officials had tried to have the fight called off, such were their fears for Carson's safety. Having beaten Halimi, Carson became the flavour of the month with London promoter Jack Solomons. Known as 'Mr Boxing', Solomons had told Carson in the dressing room, 'You did a great job for me tonight, Jimmy, I'll not forget you for it.' Carson's immediate plans lay in fighting Halimi officially for his world title, which would have netted him well in excess of £2,000. For fight fans in Belfast, however, Gilroy was the man with 'anaesthetic in his fists' and was still the best prospect for securing the British title.

Predictably, the Belfast press talked up the prospect of a Gilroy vs.

Carson clash, but that was a contest for the future. With Docherty offering Gilroy a three-figure payday (£100) for a second outing in Glasgow, the fight with Gasperini was his number-one priority. By fight night, yet again, Gilroy would be forced to face a substitute – the fifth time an opponent had cried off before a clash with the Irishman. The replacement for the Glasgow fight was the Moroccan-born Spaniard Jose Alvarez. Incredibly, Alvarez's record stood at fought sixteen, won one, lost fifteen. His only win had been recorded when his opponent had been disqualified. For those Glaswegians in attendance – and, indeed, for those from Belfast who had made the long trip by boat and bus – it was, on paper, a farce of a match. Gilroy was in a no-win situation against a man whose ability in the ring was limited to say the least.

Not surprisingly, Freddie won the fight after four and a half one-sided rounds. The punch that did the final damage was again a left hook, which sent Alvarez across the ring in a daze and onto his back. Up until then, though, Gilroy had been ineffective against an oppo-nent who had used his cunning to frustrate the Belfast man. The fight was a reality check for Gilroy, as the large crowd witnessed nothing to suggest that they were watching a contender to Keenan's crown. It was also a pyrrhic victory, as Gilroy picked up an injury to his left hand which effectively put him out of boxing for three months.

For Sam Docherty, the bill just about broke even in financial terms, with the crowd barely topping fifteen thousand. Both Keenan and Brown won their bouts against their stand-in opponents. Gilroy's clash with Alvarez had been a learning experience without glory, which had provided Jimmy McAree with food for thought. With an injured left hand to contend with, McAree told the press that any lay-off his boxer would endure would give him the opportunity to develop his right hand. That, he added, 'would help him to prove that he wasn't just a one-handed boxer, as the critics had claimed'.

With offers of fights coming in swiftly throughout the summer break, the Gilroy camp carefully considered its next move. Talk of a clash with Jimmy Carson would have been a Belfast promoter's dream. However, such a fight would, in late 1957, not have been beneficial for either boxer. With his defeat of Halimi, Carson could now demand big money to appear, and his manager, Frank McAloran, was keen to cash in on the Continent, given his boxer's newly found fame. A fight with Gilroy would have been a step backwards. Therefore, whilst both McAree and McAloran talked up a fight between Gilroy and Carson, it was mere tittle-tattle.

With Freddie's hand in the process of healing, McAree agreed to test him at a bill scheduled for Belle Vue, Manchester on 6 September. His opponent was to be the promising Eric Brett. All was not proceeding to plan with Gilroy's injury, though, so McAree took the decision to withdraw his man a week prior to the fight to allow more healing time. Legendary Glentoran Football Club physiotherapist Bobby McGregor was now treating the injury.

A comeback fight for Gilroy was agreed for Saturday 5 October in the King's Hall against – yet again – Rudy Edwards. Edwards had given Peter Keenan a tremendous fight in Glasgow in August and it seemed that he would pose a few testing questions to Gilroy. In somewhat predictable fashion, promoter George Connell received a telegram five days before the fight to say that Edwards had 'influenza and would not be fit'. With twelve thousand tickets already sold for the King's Hall, it fell to Belfast's George O'Neill to fill in at the last moment. O'Neill, who had enjoyed a proud record as an amateur and professional, had, since losing to Keenan in the King's Hall in 1954, fought on ten occasions, losing seven times. His was a career which had long since peaked.

Against Gilroy, O'Neill put up a brave display but was stopped in the seventh round. Gilroy was a restless bundle of energy, and it looked as if the fight would not go beyond the second as O'Neill was exposed to sweeping left hooks to the body and head. With blood pouring from his opponent's left eye, Gilroy went looking for the decisive punch in the seventh and forced the referee, Andy McDowell, to step in to stop proceedings. Beaten but not disgraced, was how the press described O'Neill's performance. His pluck and experience kept him in the contest, but eventually Gilroy's firepower shone through.

The fight had come at a cost for Gilroy, as his left hand had once again been damaged. Fears that he had cracked a knuckle were soon discounted when severe ligament damage was diagnosed. Gilroy was again laid up and his fighting exploits for 1957 were at an end. In November, a paid debut in London had to be turned down; promoter Harry 'the Horse' Levine had offered a substantial fee to secure Gilroy for his bill in the Royal Albert Hall. A return to the King's Hall on 23 November was also ruled out by the injury. The fans felt somewhat short-changed.

It had been a whirlwind start for Gilroy in 1957, and 1958 promised to be even better. However, questions were now being asked about Gilroy's persistent injury to his left hand and, indeed, his stamina. He was by no means the finished article.

As the new year dawned, Gilroy's hand injury was slow to heal. However, a frustrating lay-off ended on 8 March 1958, when he met the cautious but capable Belgian Pierre Cossemyns at the King's Hall. The clash with Cossemyns, who was rated as number five in Europe, was a true step up for Gilroy. The Belgian had lost previously on points to Hogan Bassey, who had then gone on to claim the world featherweight title. And for Belfast boxing fans, Cossemyns was well-remembered as the man who had shattered the career of Belfast favourite John Kelly with a venomous right hook at the King's Hall in 1954. The doom merchants were predicting that Gilroy's climb through the bantamweight rankings would come to an abrupt end. 'I know that it will be a hard fight,' said Gilroy. 'But it is my job to fight good fighters, not "has-beens" from whom I wouldn't learn a thing.'

Caution was the order of the day as Gilroy's camp added John Kelly as chief sparring partner to assist in preparations for the fight. Questions were again asked about Gilroy's hand and whether it had healed properly. 'It's as hard as a rock,' claimed Gilroy. 'Jimmy McAree will verify that. I have been hammering a heavy punchbag a lot recently and there's not been a twinge of pain – on 8 March that will be the same case.' The fight with the Belgian was a calculated risk for Gilroy, who, as a relative novice, was to face a comparative veteran of fifty-five contests.

The Gilroy-Cossemyns fight would be the main supporting contest to Billy 'Spider' Kelly's British lightweight title eliminator against George Martin. Kelly remained the darling of the King's Hall, but his career was most definitely on the wane. Regardless, the Belfast and Derry fans snapped up tickets in their thousands.

On the night itself, Gilroy made no mistakes. Sitting ringside to witness the pretender to his crown was Peter Keenan, who must have been impressed by what he witnessed. Gilroy pounded the Belgian around the King's Hall ring to satisfied roars from the capacity crowd. After three rounds of hooks and jabs, Gilroy upped the ante and opened up with body shots which almost sent the Belgian through the ropes. Referee Billy Duncan stepped in to administer a count; he had to manhandle Gilroy away from his prey. When the referee shouted 'box on', Gilroy pinned his opponent into a neutral corner and finished the job, leaving Cossemyns a gasping heap. Within seconds, Gilroy was dancing a victory jig in the ring. He had returned with style. Keenan took detailed notes from his ringside seat.

To round off a great night for local boxers, Kelly won his eliminator on points, which meant there was a distinct possibility that both he and Gilroy would have British title bouts in Belfast. Promoter George Connell was, unsurprisingly, upbeat about that prospect. 'Kelly and Gilroy are in the glaring limelight now and the local public want to see them,' he told the press. 'I have big plans for both – and

I am very hard to beat in a bidding war.' The press was now adding to Gilroy's nicknames by calling him 'Mr Box Office'. In the space of a year, Gilroy had gone from the Clouting Cherub and the Clubbing Choirboy to Mr Box Office. Life in the paid-fight game was, so far, pretty good for the Ardoyne man.

6.

CALDWELL GOES WITH THE MONEY

When Freddie Gilroy made the jump into the paid ranks in January 1957, rumours abounded that John Caldwell would follow suit. John, however, wasn't ready for such a step up. He needed time to mature in both body and style before he could take the leap of faith into the professional game. John was an all-action boxer who had been open to punishment as he tired in the last rounds of his contests. Seasoned observers had noted that his stamina was suspect. At merely eighteen years of age, he had plenty of time to address that flaw.

Besides, a crack at any meaningful professional title would have to wait until he reached the age of majority, three years hence. With the European championships taking place in Prague in May and internationals against England, Germany and Italy in the offing, John heeded the wise advice provided to him and decided to remain an amateur. He was enjoying the adoration in his native Belfast, and 1957 promised more travel, adulation and glory. The man who had been eagerly chasing Caldwell's signature, Glasgow promoter Sam Docherty, was told politely to bide his time and put away his chequebook; Caldwell wasn't ready.

John duly made himself available for the crucial international between Ireland and England scheduled for the Royal Albert Hall on 30 January. With the uncertainty surrounding Caldwell's future, the IABA had chosen the army private Tony 'Mousie' Connolly for the flyweight spot, but he sportingly stood aside to allow the Olympian to take his place. The bill was a sell-out, as the reputation the Irish team had gained in Melbourne attracted multitudes to the south London venue. The event was screened live on BBC television.

Topping the bill that night was the clash between Tony Byrne and Olympic champion Dick McTaggart. Byrne boxed the gangly champion with a ferocity seldom seen in an amateur ring. In the second round, he caught McTaggart with a savage right hand, which forced the referee to intervene and administer a count of eight. In the last round, McTaggart fought back but Byrne held on to claim a worthy victory, which had crowds dancing with glee on the streets of Drogheda. For Caldwell, it was a case of daylight robbery, as Derek Lloyd took a hotly disputed decision over him. While Lloyd did give the Irish champion a tough fight, John's two-handed style left him a clear winner in the eyes of the crowd. The verdict was greeted with prolonged, slow hand-clapping and left a sour taste in the mouths of the considerable Irish contingent. The tournament ended in a four-all draw. It was deemed one of the most entertaining internationals seen in many years.

The setback against Lloyd did not outwardly affect Caldwell. In his next two outings, against visiting German sides in Derry and Dublin, he saw off Felix Hendrix twice. Then he retained his Irish title with a win over Peter Lavery of the St John Bosco club at the National Stadium on Friday, 23 March. That win secured him a place on the Irish team that met a strong Italian side twice in the space of five days in early April. In his clash with Salvatore Manca in Dublin, John was forced to ship a series of looping right hands, which caused consternation in the National Stadium. However, it was his ability to counter and punish the Italian on the retreat which earned Caldwell his win and set Ireland on its way to a 6–4 victory.

In the Ulster Hall on 9 April, it was a different story, as Ireland endured an 8–2 reversal, with Caldwell and Des Leahy recording Ireland's only victories in an off night for the men in green. The scene was now set, in theory, for Caldwell to take gold for Ireland at the European Championships in Prague, where he had been installed as the hot favourite.

After the brilliance of the Melbourne Olympic Games, Ireland's performance at the 1957 European championships was disappointing, to say the least. Finance was again a problem for the IABA, and a team of only four boxers was chosen for the trip: Caldwell, Tiedt, Michael Reid and Peter Bourke. After competing in the United States, Canada and Australia, Prague was a totally different experience for John and the Irish team. Accommodation and food were humble and the reality of post-war communism came as an eye-opener for the Irish team.

Caldwell was pitted against the West German Manfred Homberg on the opening day of the tournament and was expected to win easily. In the first round, however, John slipped while breaking from a clinch, and the referee adjudged it to have been a knock-down and administered a count of eight. Thereafter, John dished out punishment at will to Homberg, whose face was covered in blood as the bell rang to finish the bout. The referee's count proved to be John's undoing, though. With four judges split evenly between the two boxers, it fell to the referee to administer the coup de grâce to Caldwell, awarding the contest to the German. It was a demoralising blow, and it effectively convinced Caldwell that it was time to consider the professional game. Ireland's only success at the tournament came through Tiedt, who boxed his way to the semi-finals to claim a bronze medal.

On John's return to Belfast, moves were made behind the scenes to heal the rift between him and Jack McCusker. The men had a deep bond and John wanted the security of McCusker by his side when he turned professional. Loyalty and friendship were the keys to the future partnership between John and Jack and, eventually, hands were shaken and the prodigal son returned to the Immaculata in September 1957. The truth was that the trust which had existed before their split was never to be rebuilt. Still, a draft contract was drawn up for a seven-year agreement between Caldwell and McCusker, with McCusker entitled to a quarter of the boxer's earnings. Sam Docherty went into overdrive to secure an agreement to promote Caldwell's professional career in Glasgow.

Caldwell was nearly done with amateur boxing. In the autumn of 1957, he fulfilled a long-standing promise to the Garda team and boxed for them three times in Germany, winning all of his contests. In December, he fought his last international in a green vest when he beat Irish-born England representative Eugene O'Callaghan to finish 1957 with a record of only two defeats in sixteen contests. On 15 January 1958, John Caldwell boxed his last fight as an amateur, at the Down and Connor seniors' tournament in St Mary's Hall in Belfast's Bank Street. His opponent, Peter Lavery, would go on to claim a bronze medal at the Cardiff Commonwealth Games that year and enjoy a distinguished career. That night he played his part in what was a classic bout filled with speed, skill and determination. Caldwell, though, was a clear winner, rounding off an amateur career which had seen him lose only six contests in 243 fights and claim twenty-four titles.

The night was all about Caldwell's momentous announcement, which was left to Captain T. D. Morrison, president of the Ulster Council of the IABA, to relay to the crowd. When the applause for Caldwell and Lavery subsided, Morrison took the microphone and the crowd fell silent. Jack Magowan noted in the *Belfast Telegraph* that 'Morrison's voice was not entirely free of emotion' as he announced:

It is with utmost regret that I have to tell you that John Caldwell has fought his last amateur fight . . . He has fought for Ireland so many times – and won so many times for Ireland – that we shall miss him. But I feel that I am expressing the wish of every boxing fan when I say good luck, John, we wish you every success in the professional ranks.

The silence of the hall was replaced by long and enthusiastic applause, as the Belfast fight fans saluted Caldwell. Magowan noted in the *Belfast Telegraph* that he would eat his hat if Caldwell had not proved himself as Britain's top flyweight within eighteen months.

The best-kept secret in Irish boxing had finally been revealed. Caldwell and McCusker were now a formal partnership, prolonging a nine-year relationship which had seen Caldwell hit the heights of world amateur boxing. Caldwell's job as an apprentice plumber would not be sacrificed immediately for the professional fight game, but money was now the primary aim of his boxing, and he would soon find out that there would be trainers, intermediaries, matchmakers, bookmakers, hardmen, crooks and hangers-on willing to take cuts of his earnings. And Jack McCusker would soon discover that he was too much of a gentleman to be a manager in professional boxing.

Sam Docherty was the man who stood poised to take the reins of Caldwell's career. Docherty had been a naval officer and a prize-fighter before he had gone on to make a fortune as a bookmaker. He had made a name for himself as a promoter in the early 1950s, when he had staged Glasgow bantamweight Peter Keenan's British and European title fights against Londoner Dickie O'Sullivan and Spaniard Luis Romero before crowds of forty thousand at Firhill Park. He was a shrewd man who knew exactly how much of a money-spinner Caldwell would become, especially in Glasgow, with its tens of thousands of inhabitants of Irish descent. In essence, Docherty wanted to manage – not promote – Caldwell and, with

Keenan's career in its twilight, he believed he had the clout to secure the Belfast boxer for himself. McCusker was the man with the contract with Caldwell, but Docherty had time on his hands, when it came to securing the Belfast boxer for himself.

Docherty fixed Caldwell's debut for Wednesday, 5 February 1958 at Glasgow's Kelvin Hall, against twenty-four-year-old Billy Downer from Stoke Newington. In the newspapers that evening, the main sporting story was Manchester United's 3–3 draw against Red Star Belgrade, which saw United through to the semi-finals of the European Cup for the first time ever. The journey homewards was to end tragically for the United team and its entourage on Thursday, 6 February, when the dreadful story of the Munich air crash began to unfold. That tragedy would fill the front and back pages of the world's papers in the following days and weeks.

By a quarter past eight on the evening of 5 February, Caldwell was making his way through a subdued crowd to begin his career within the paid ranks. He was greeted with warm applause as he was introduced to the crowd, with McCusker standing proud in his corner and Docherty a very interested ringside figure. Downer had enjoyed an unspectacular career as a flyweight, losing twenty of his thirty-three contests, and was not expected to give Caldwell much of a test.

Those expectations were fulfilled as the bell rang and Caldwell went at Downer, landing with flurry after flurry of punches. When the referee stepped in to stop the contest in the second round there was a buzz of appreciation amongst the Glasgow crowd at the efficient manner in which Caldwell had dispatched his opponent. Docherty was glowing in his praise of Caldwell to the media, as he held court after the fight. Predicting that John would be a British champion, Docherty added, 'I am flattered that Caldwell made his professional debut for me. His style appeals to the Glasgow fight fans and I hope they will be seeing him a lot more this year.' Such was Docherty's eagerness to oversee Caldwell's progress that, before the boxer went home to Belfast, Docherty secured his signature for his next promotion, on 5 March.

Caldwell's opponent at the Kelvin Hall that March night was Doncaster's Eddie Barraclough, a twenty-year-old who had a record of nine fights, of which he had won just four. Barraclough was a spirited boxer who would go on to be ranked in the top ten of the British flyweight division between 1959 and 1962. However, he was not in Caldwell's class and lasted less than two minutes, as John came out with all guns blazing. That victory only added to Caldwell's reputation in the British flyweight class, and it was obvious that most boxers were reluctant to face the man who was nicknamed the Killer by the Glasgow press. Add to that the premature comparisons between Caldwell and Irish legend Rinty Monaghan, and it was obvious that it was a risky step for any aspiring British boxer to face the Belfast man.

On 21 May, Docherty promoted Caldwell and Gilroy on the same bill in Glasgow, and they brought a considerable Irish contingent to the city. Caldwell was made to work hard for a victory on points over the Frenchman Moncer Sahri. Gilroy, fresh from his emphatic victory over Pierre Cossemyns, reinforced his title credentials with an emphatic win over Kimpo Armarfio of Ghana. Docherty's dream would have been to manage both Caldwell and Gilroy, but Jack McCusker and Jimmy McAree stood firm against the financial flattery of the Glasgow bookmaker. Gilroy's win again reinforced his claims on Keenan's title, and expectations were high that a title eliminator was not too far off.

Caldwell fought his fourth paid fight on 18 June and stopped France's Michel Lamora after four energy-filled rounds. For Caldwell, though, it was a victory at a cost, as he injured his left shoulder during one of his onslaughts against the Frenchman. It was an injury that ended Caldwell's fighting for the summer period. It had been an impressive four months for John, and Sam Docherty's big plan for him was taking shape, slowly but surely.

7.

FREDDIE CLOSES IN ON KEENAN

Soon after his win over Amarfio, the British Boxing Board paired Gilroy with Hartlepool's George Bowes in an eliminator for Keenan's title. It was not a *final* eliminator, but a victory would, in theory, guarantee the Belfast man a fight with Keenan for his crown in the autumn. The fight was fixed for the Engineers Club in West Hartlepool on Monday, 30 June. Bowes had turned professional under manager Terry Allen less than a year earlier and had won eleven of his twelve contests, drawing the twelfth. A former coal miner, he had been nicknamed the Bomber and possessed a powerful punch, which had stopped nine of his opponents. He was tall for a bantamweight, but possessed a watertight defence. Both men were unbeaten in their paid careers and promoter Walter Hazeltine had rewarded Gilroy with a 'substantial' sum to fight in Hartlepool. Gilroy was taking a big chance by going into Bowes's hometown to meet the challenge. Sixty fans from Belfast made the ferry-and-coach trip through Yorkshire to see their hero and, as expected, made their presence quite audible at ringside.

The fight, in front of six thousand fans, was close, but Gilroy did enough to shade the decision. In the third round, he piled on the pressure and connected with a crisp left hook that sent Bowes to the floor for the first time in his paid career. Bowes recovered to take the fight to Gilroy but was slower to the punch and, as the fight wore on, he tired as Gilroy gained momentum. Subsequent to the fight, it was discovered that Bowes had incurred a hairline fracture to his left ankle. Doctors were dumbfounded as to how he had picked up this injury and fought on despite the pain. It was later acknowledged by medics – and by none other than Bowes himself – that the power of the punch which had floored him in the third round had reverberated throughout his body, fracturing his ankle as it exited. Gilroy's splendid punching power needed no better affirmation.

Sitting at ringside had been the champion, Keenan, who now knew that it was only a matter of time until his clash with Gilroy. However, the British Boxing Board procrastinated in ordering Keenan to defend his crown and, to the dismay of Jimmy McAree and Gilroy, decreed that Gilroy had to fight a final eliminator. Standing in Gilroy's way for a crack at Keenan's title was Motherwell's Johnny Morrisey, whom Gilroy had beaten during his amateur career.

Docherty staged the contest on 17 September and labelled it the fight of the year. He had no difficulty selling tickets for the Kelvin Hall bill to eager fans in Glasgow and Belfast. In characteristic style, he promised to 'pull out all the stops' to match the winner of the bout with world champion Alphonse Halimi – in Glasgow, no less. It was, of course, mere rhetoric. But it did sell tickets. In the days before the bout, Docherty had the Kelvin Hall's layout changed to accommodate an additional two thousand seats, with half of those required for Belfast fans.

Morrisey, a twenty-year-old plumber, had enjoyed a fine amateur record and, like Gilroy, had had a meteoric rise through the British rankings. Having won eleven of his twelve contests, Morrisey had notably taken the scalps of Belfast's George O'Neill and Jimmy

Carson, as well as stopping the rated Spaniard Antonio Diaz in three rounds. Crude, menacing, and filled with stamina, Morrisey was a fighter who possessed a fearsome punch and had the ability to hurt his opponents. However, so too had Freddie Gilroy.

Two weeks prior to the clash, an X-ray of Gilroy's left hand showed no damage, and he was deemed fit to box. The uncertainty of the twelve months of what Freddie described as 'a toothache' in his hand was over, and the twenty-two-year-old was ready for his toughest match to date. With Belfast fighters Gilroy, Carson and Caldwell appearing on the bill, together with Derry's Billy 'Spider' Kelly, the early-morning boats from Belfast to Glasgow were brimming with Irish fight fans.

In the background, the predestined fall-out between John Caldwell and Jack McCusker was moving ever closer, as Sam Docherty's grip on the boxer tightened. On 17 July 1958, Caldwell had married his childhood sweetheart, Bridie Maguire, in Glasgow, and the couple began looking for accommodation in the city. Since his win over Lamora in June, Caldwell had been under Docherty's personal care, staying at Docherty's plush house under the watchful eye of his wife, Jean.

Making sure Caldwell was in bed each night at ten, with two bottles of Guinness administered daily to build him up, Jean Docherty took on the role of surrogate mother. McCusker remained, in name only, John's manager; anyone could see that that relationship was in difficulties. In Glasgow, Joe Aitcheson, a tough disciplinarian, had taken on the role of Caldwell's trainer. Docherty was now calling the shots for a man who, at twenty, remained a precocious talent but could not legally fight for a title.

On the night of Gilroy's fight with Morrisey, Caldwell made his mark emphatically with a cool, calculated performance, outpointing the rugged little springbok Dennis Adams. Caldwell's victory was notable, as Adams held the British Empire crown and had been beaten by a man too young even to fight for a professional title. The fight was by no means a classic – a fact blamed on poor refereeing and spoiling tactics by Adams. To his credit, however, Caldwell kept his opponent at range, punching with his left as opposed to mixing his combinations. To many in the Glasgow crowd, Caldwell resembled their own pre-war hero Benny Lynch as he took every round and lashed his way through Adams's flailing defence. His ability in the ring was plain for all to see as he pounded away at the South African, who survived a last-round onslaught during which he was mostly pinned against the ropes. Writing after the fight in the *News of the World*, the legendary Welsh heavyweight Tommy Farr described Caldwell as potentially the best flyweight he had seen since Benny Lynch's days. For Docherty, it was proof that he had been promoting what was, potentially, a veritable gold mine in John Caldwell.

For Carson, it was another night of disappointment, as Eric Betts stopped him in two rounds by giving him a serious cut over his right eye. The victory over Halimi was proving to have been a freak result for Carson, and his career was waning as Gilroy and Caldwell grew in stature. For Kelly, it was to be yet another frustrating night. In his lightweight battle against Gracia, he seemed to be in control until blood trickled from his left eye in the ninth round. The cut worsened and the referee was forced to intervene.

The Kelvin Hall was packed with fourteen thousand raucous fans as Gilroy entered the ring to face the local hero, Morrisey. There was, of course, history between the two boxers, who had met in an Ireland vs. Scotland international in October 1956. On that occasion, Gilroy had been victorious, but the Scot had come on strong in the last round and had almost shaded the decision. The fact that Caldwell had been sparring with Morrisey in preparation for the fight was another factor that gave an edge to the proceedings, from Gilroy's perspective; he was not happy that Caldwell had been assisting his opponent.

It was, however, to be Morrisey's thirteenth professional fight, which some took as a bad omen. Gilroy looked to be in fabulous shape as he controlled the early exchanges. He dictated the fight, making Morrisey look third-rate with a work rate that was perfect. That continued until the seventh round, when Gilroy walked into a vicious uppercut from Morrisey that sent him to the floor amid a roar that would have made even Hampden Park shudder. Many lesser fighters would have stayed down from the punch, but Gilroy bounced back up. Distressed and gasping for breath, his jelly-like legs fought to regain their balance. Morrisey was primed and went for the kill but could not catch the Belfast boxer again as the bell sounded to end what had been a disastrous round for Gilroy.

In round eight, Gilroy fought back to regain the advantage. The Irish contingent were going wild as life poured back into Gilroy's chunky body, and he battled with abandon, throwing flurry after flurry of punches. Eventually, with seconds left in the round, Gilroy connected with a picture-perfect left hand, which sent Morrisey to the floor in apparent agony. A sickening crack of lethal leather against static bone was lost in the delirious roar of the Belfast fans. As the bell sounded, a prostrate Morrisey indicated with his gloves that he had been hurt badly. 'I'm finished, I can't go on. I think I've smashed my jaw,' he screamed to his corner from the floor.

Morrisey had, indeed, suffered a broken jaw and it was left to Welsh referee Ike Powell to raise Gilroy's hand in triumph. Belfast-style pandemonium erupted, as medics raced to treat the distressed and beaten Scot. It was a tearful Morrisey who was taken to hospital, accompanied by his distraught wife, Margaret, who had witnessed the destructive punch from her ringside seat. 'Slowly, perceptively, he was reduced from a cedar to a cinder in the most powerful ambush he has yet known,' reported Jack Magowan in the *Belfast Telegraph*.

Gilroy was now officially the number-one contender for Keenan's title and odds-on favourite to win it. Belfast promoter George Connell had lunch with Keenan in Glasgow on the day after Gilroy's clash with Morrisey and was told abruptly by Britain's longest-reigning champion that he would require a king's ransom to box Gilroy in Belfast. Negotiations were protracted, with Keenan holding out for a payday that would see him comfortable in retirement.

Gilroy and Caldwell were scheduled to box a pair of Spaniards on Docherty's next promotion on 29 October. Gilroy was paired that evening with Jose Martinez. It was to be a warm-up fight ahead of the Keenan clash, but the manner of his victory was vital. The old injury to Gilroy's left hand had flared up again since the Morrisey fight, and McAree had been reluctant to take on the Martinez fight. It was a below-par Gilroy who was awarded the decision over eight rounds, much to the consternation of the Glasgow audience. The decision was greeted with boos and a slow handclap. Gilroy's performance called into question his ability to win Keenan's title. It was a setback for Gilroy, who had weighed in at an eye-opening 8st 8lb, meaning that he had gained almost 6lb in just over a month. John Caldwell's fight with Junito Cid at the Kelvin Hall ended in the fifth round with a punch that knocked the Spaniard out cold. It was an easy victory for the Belfast boy, although he shipped a strong left hook in the third round.

Negotiations between the Gilroy and Keenan camps continued. There was to be no early resolution, and the Gilroy camp returned to Belfast without a contract. In the interim, Keenan had opted to take a lucrative payday in a non-title fight with Alphonse Halimi in Paris in November. It seemed that the champion wanted to cash in on his fame before he faced up to the challenge of Gilroy.

On 29 November, Caldwell returned to make his first appearance as a professional in front of a Belfast audience, when he met Esteban Martin of Paris at the King's Hall. His debut outside Glasgow must have worried Sam Docherty, who cancelled a holiday in Barcelona to be ringside in Belfast. Still acting merely as Caldwell's 'mentor', Docherty's links with the Belfast boxer were tenuous. A debut under promoter George Connell in front of an adoring Belfast crowd could only impinge on Docherty's financial plans for the flyweight. He was keeping his eye on Caldwell both inside and – more importantly – outside the Belfast ring.

The King's Hall bill was again topped by Spider Kelly, who was to lose against Belgium's Louis Van Hoeck. A majority of the crowd of ten thousand, though, were there to see Caldwell. Gilroy had originally been scheduled to box the German Alfred Schweer on the bill, but Jimmy McAree had forbidden Gilroy to fight while discussions continued with Keenan. Belfast boxing was on a high and, with Gilroy now standing on the cusp of a British title, the prospect of Caldwell's appearance drew the Falls Road supporters in their droves. Writing in the *Belfast Telegraph*, Jack Magowan described Caldwell's style thus: 'he's like a wasp at a picnic, tireless, vigilant, always looking for trouble'. Caldwell put in a confident performance over ten rounds and outpointed Martin with ease. It was not spectacular by any means, but his perpetual motion throughout and crisp punching was well received by the appreciative crowd. It was Caldwell's seventh straight win.

Belfast could hardly wait for 1959. On 7 May, Caldwell – the Cold-Eyed Killer – would turn twenty-one, making him eligible for a crack at Frankie Jones's British flyweight title. And Connell would eventually come up with the king's ransom to make the Gilroy vs. Keenan fight happen. At stake would be Keenan's British and Empire bantamweight titles.

8.

KEENAN MEETS HIS MATCH

On 17 November 1958, Peter Keenan stepped into the ring to face world champion Alphonse Halimi in a non-title fight at the Palais des Sports in Paris. It was a fairly lucrative bout for the thirty-year-old, who knew that his career was coming to an end but was determined to go out on a positive note. That was the plan. It was to be a horrendous half-hour in the ring for the proud Scot. Without mercy, Halimi hammered Keenan senseless in front of eighteen thousand spectators, taking all ten rounds with consummate ease. Speaking afterwards to the press, Keenan, his face battered and bloodied, denied that he was going to retire. He then winked at the reporters, telling them, 'I am ready for Freddie Gilroy.'

In early December 1958, with negotiations for the Gilroy-Keenan fight dragging on, the British Boxing Board intervened and ordered the champion to defend his title against Gilroy by no later than the middle of January. The fight was secured by Connell for the King's Hall on Saturday, 10 January; Keenan's signature had been obtained with a promise of a £4,000 cheque. For Connell, it was a fight that was too good to miss out on, given that a bumper crowd of seventeen thousand at the King's Hall was a certainty, together with lucrative television and radio royalties, which would more than cover his costs. It was promoted as Perky Peter against the Clouting Cherub for the British and Empire bantamweight titles, and the Belfast public was captivated by the prospect.

One issue, however, which was beginning to come again to the fore with Gilroy, was his weight. It was no secret that Freddie loved his fish and chips, cakes and ice cream, and Jimmy McAree put the bantamweight on a strict caveman diet of steak and salads to make the agreed 8st 6lb limit. There was to be no Christmas dinner for Gilroy in 1958, as salads replaced turkey and trimmings. Sparring for Freddie in the Bosco gym was carried out over sixteen rounds each day with Peter Lavery, Jim Jordan and Sean Brown as top-class opponents. Add to that a gruelling ten-mile run each morning around Belfast's picturesque Cave Hill, and soon Gilroy was determined and focussed on the task ahead.

With a week left before the fight, Connell announced that all of the one-, two- and four-guinea seats at the King's Hall had been sold out and that additional seats would be installed in the spacious balcony. 'If the King's Hall was twice its size, we could still fill it,' he said. Modern health-and-safety practitioners would have encountered cardiac problems if they had inspected the hall that week. The previous record gate of fourteen thousand would be exceeded by at least three thousand spectators. However, nobody will ever know how many people were actually present in the arena on 10 January 1959.

The fight was the first 'international' contest held between Irish and Scottish boxers at the venue since the post-fight riot which had marred the defeat of Billy Kelly by Charlie Hill in 1956. Connell, anxious to avoid any further scenes of anarchy, had employed three hundred stewards to manage the crowd in the event of an upset in the ring. In addition to the pressure on Gilroy, there was most definitely pressure on the promoter to keep the peace. Helping to ease

Connell's money worries, the BBC had paid him handsomely for the rights to film exclusive highlights of the fight. Connell, who had steadfastly refused to allow the fight to be televised, had soon changed his mind when a full house had been assured. Stating that he had decided to allow the cameras into the venue because 'it would be a pity to deny so many old people the chance to share in the thrills', Connell had negotiated a four-figure sum with the BBC.

Keenan had a personal reason to beat Gilroy. Having won two Lonsdale Belts – a feat that had secured him a pension of £2 a week for life from the British Boxing Board – he had given one each to his children Peter junior and Anne. His youngest, Yvonne, had also been promised a belt. To fulfil this promise, victory in Belfast was essential. However, with Keenan having first claimed the British title in 1951, most observers felt that his visit to Belfast would bring the end of his career; Gilroy was the overwhelming favourite. Keenan was a wealthy man, with an estimated £50,000 earned throughout his career and a significant property portfolio. He told the press he would retire if Gilroy beat him; perhaps, in his own mind, he had lost the fight already.

Gilroy had been attending hospital for treatment of his hands for almost a year, and he was ordered not to shake hands with well-wishers in the six weeks prior to the fight. His preparations were painstaking, with roadwork commencing religiously at 6.30 each morning. Into his black book each day, McAree pencilled meticulously everything Gilroy ate, every mile he ran, every round he sparred and, most crucially, every ounce of weight he lost: nothing was being left to chance. Speaking to the media, Gilroy was low-key, paying tribute to Keenan as a legendary champion and refusing to predict the outcome.

The weigh-in took place in the Ulster Hall on Friday morning, 9 January, and almost 1,500 fans turned up to see the proceedings. Acting as doorman, the well-known Belfast hardman Barney Wilson senior struggled to keep the unlucky fans outside the hall. Indeed, things almost got out of hand, and the police were called as Wilson handed out countless thick ears to punters who were over-eager to get in. Freddie weighed in well under the limit at almost 8st 4lb, while Keenan came in just a fraction under the weight. The talk among the spectators was all of a Gilroy victory, with some predicting – despite the fact that he and Caldwell were fighting at different weights – that a first defence against Caldwell would be a fitting gesture.

With most of Belfast praying for a Gilroy win, one person admitted that she would forgo a ringside seat and, indeed, would not be listening to the live radio coverage of the fight. Mrs May Gilroy, Freddie's mother, told Bill Rutherford in the *People*, 'I have never seen him fight and I never want to see him fight.' The rest of Belfast thought differently, and on 10 January the Lisburn Road was thronged with crowds from early lunchtime in anticipation of a piece of Gilroy magic. Having queued for over twelve hours to get the best seats in the balcony, Belfast brothers Jack and Clarke Donald were cold but undaunted in the queue outside the arena, saying, 'We wouldn't have missed the fight for the world.'

A last minute fall-out between the camps was averted when the British Boxing Board intervened and ordered Gilroy to wear modified shorts with light stripes sewn down the sides, to avoid a clash with Keenan's colours. Gilroy's 'lucky' black-and-red shorts had been given to him by Bosco clubmate Sean Brown prior to the start of his professional career. Regardless of the colour of the stripes on the shorts, though, Gilroy was ready for his biggest challenge.

The bill Connell put on in support of the Gilroy-Keenan fight was an attractive one. The chief supporting bout would see Caldwell face France's Simon Carnazza over ten rounds. It was appropriate that Caldwell would share the limelight on Gilroy's big night. With the bill broadcast on the BBC, Caldwell would be assured massive exposure to a British and Irish audience. His opponent had not recorded a victory since March 1956. Caldwell barely broke a sweat as he toyed with the Frenchman, forcing him to retire at the end of the fifth round. Showered, suited and booted, the Cold-Eyed Killer was installed beside Docherty at ringside as Freddie Gilroy entered the arena to a deafening roar; Keenan must have shuddered as the noise reverberated around his dressing room.

Whether due to the ageing Scottish champion's fear, age or indifference, the predictions of his defeat proved correct. In the third round, Gilroy opened up forcefully on the champion, whose years of experience were deserting him as his youthful opponent caught him with ease. Keenan stumbled and went to the canvas for the first time in the fight. Pride brought him to his feet.

Twice Keenan was toppled in the eighth round, but it was the eleventh that brought his ultimate downfall. Gilroy floored him, then again, and again, as the champion was bounced from rope to rope amid a ferocious noise from the hometown fans. While Gilroy was showing no mercy, the referee felt obliged to administer his own compassion to Keenan. With a mere second of the round remaining, and Keenan pinned to the bottom ropes, referee Billy Williams stepped in to end the slaughter.

The Scot had been hammered and pounded pitilessly into submission. He was a sorry sight, with his right ear a cauliflower-shaped, purple shell; he later required hospital treatment for a perforated eardrum. Gilroy had been merciless in his destruction. It was a rout, and Gilroy was the new champion. At just twenty-two, he had taken the British and Empire titles in the most emphatic style. 'He stuck to him like an unshakeable shadow,' noted Jack Magowan in the *Belfast Telegraph*.

The ring invasion began in earnest to salute Gilroy. The scenes of unrelenting joy prompted the seventeen-thousand-strong crowd into a rendition of 'When Irish Eyes Are Smiling'. Keenan, to his credit, embraced Gilroy and showed him off to the fans, adorned in what was now Gilroy's Lonsdale Belt. The Scot joined in with the singing, and the fans struck up 'Auld Lang Syne' and 'I Belong to Glasgow' in his honour.

To warm cheers and applause, Keenan took to the microphone to announce his retirement. He knew that he had been beaten by a better boxer and puncher. His era was at an end, and he signed off to a sporting acclamation worthy of his fine career. The *Daily Mirror* ran a banner headline on the Monday after the fight: HE WENT OUT ON THE WORST BEATING OF HIS CAREER. Speaking after the fight in a silent dressing room, Keenan said he hoped Gilroy would hold the titles for as long as he had done – and make as much money.

In Ardoyne, crowds poured onto the streets to celebrate Gilroy's victory. As the sudden cries of joy resounded in the tight terraced streets, May Gilroy knew that her son had been victorious. She blessed herself and left the silence of her bedroom. Despite the snow on the ground, a celebratory bonfire was assembled in the middle of Northwick Drive, and everything that was not nailed down was thrust onto the pyre. By half eleven that evening, hundreds were still singing and partying in the streets as Freddie and his manager, Jimmy McAree, walked casually down Northwick Drive, almost unannounced. They had slipped out of the King's Hall with Freddie's father and brother, Ted, to escape the madness. 'I just wanted to loosen up,' Freddie told amazed reporters. The celebrations went on late into the night, and the remnants of countless garden fences were still smouldering as Gilroy walked the next morning through Ardoyne to 11 AM Mass in the Holy Cross church.

Sitting at ringside that Saturday night as Gilroy bested Keenan and Caldwell beat Carnazza, had been Sam Docherty. He had seen Gilroy stamp his claim for a world title fight in forceful fashion. When he asked whether Jimmy McAree would be prepared to sell him a share in Gilroy's contract, Docherty was told politely 'no thank you'. Gilroy's fight with Keenan, Docherty believed, could have attracted at least thirty thousand fans to an outdoor Belfast venue. He wanted a taste of Gilroy's glory now that Keenan's career had ended. The bottom line, though, was that George Connell had a sound working relationship with Gilroy, who was happy to remain in Belfast. Docherty was out of the reckoning.

John Caldwell was shaping up to be every bit as popular and capable as Gilroy, but Docherty was merely his promoter. The power shift in British boxing had moved to Belfast, and Docherty knew that if he was going to remain a major player in professional boxing circles he needed Caldwell under contract. Caldwell's link with manager Jack McCusker was the sticking point in Docherty's plan to take Caldwell completely under his wing. McCusker still called the shots for Caldwell, and there was a bond of deep loyalty between the two – as well as a seven-year contract. Docherty feared that, amid the fantastic scenes in the King's Hall, Caldwell could opt to make Belfast his base, effectively eliminating Docherty from a lucrative equation.

As the celebrations in Belfast's Grand Central Hotel continued late into the night, Sam Docherty had some serious thinking to do.

9.

GROWING IN STATURE

Whilst the careers of both Freddie Gilroy and John Caldwell had flourished since they had turned professional, they had achieved glory only at a local level. Their fame outside of Ireland and Scotland was limited, with all but one of their fights having taken place in either Belfast or Glasgow. The place where reputations were won and lost was in the bright lights of London. In order for Gilroy and Caldwell to make the leap into boxing's big time, one man had to take an interest. That was Mr Boxing himself, top promoter Jack Solomons.

Born in London in 1900, Jack Solomons's family had made its fortune in the fish markets of the East End. Boxing was the lifeblood of the area, and Jack had tried his luck in the ring, losing his opening three fights. Wisely, he hung up his gloves and soon reinvented himself as a bookmaker and boxing promoter. He made his breakthrough as manager of Eric Boon, the British lightweight champion from 1938 to 1944, and as the proprietor of the Devonshire Club, where he matched up-and-coming London talent on his shows. 'Jolly Jack' soon gained a reputation as 'boxing's ultimate entrepreneur' – or so he liked to tell everyone.

In May 1946, he had brought the American world light heavy-weight champion Gus Lesnevich to the Harringay Arena to face Freddie Mills. Mills was beaten in that contest, but two years later, he reversed that decision at London's White City Stadium in front of forty-six thousand fans, a promotion which had grossed Solomons an estimated £3 million in takings in modern terms. Three years later, at Earl's Court, Solomons promoted the bill at which Sugar Ray Robinson lost his world middleweight title to Britain's Randolph Turpin, reinforcing Jack's reputation as Britain's number-one pro-moter. He had made a fortune through boxing and bookmaking, and everyone loved Jolly Jack. Well, just as long as they did not upset him.

By the late 1950s, Solomons effectively controlled British boxing and oversaw the careers of most of the top fighters. Despite signifi-cant criticism of boxing from within the chattering classes, Solomons had advanced the sport's mass popularity. In his autobiog-raphy *Jack Solomons Tells All*, the flamboyant millionaire related how he had been born with six fingers on each hand and two perfectly formed front teeth, something which was considered lucky in Judaism.

Proudly Jewish by birth, Solomons played upon all the stereo-types associated with being a big-time money-man, although nobody knew exactly how much he was worth. Chomping – for the sake of appearance – on the finest of Cuban cigars, Solomons was a lifelong fan of Tottenham Hotspur. His extensive bookmaking busi-ness and boxing empire were administered from a dingy office in London's Soho area. In seeking out American talent for his London bills, he incurred phone bills of up to £5,000 a month – and he boasted about such exorbitant costs. Despite all this, he was not averse to crying poverty to anyone who cared to listen.

Solomons knew everyone who was anyone, from politicians to gangsters, film stars, top policemen and businessmen. He was the man whose face adorned the front pages of programmes for his promotions. Boxers were sometimes incidental to his ego; he positively wallowed in his celebrity status. If Gilroy and Caldwell were to take the final steps onto the world stage, London was the place to be, and Jack Solomons was the man to impress.

Freddie Gilroy's growing status in the bantamweight ranks was acknowledged in February 1959, when world champion Alphonse Halimi offered £1,000 to box him in a non-title fight in Paris. McAree and Gilroy knew that Halimi had hammered Peter Keenan in similar circumstances in Paris three months previously, and wisely turned down the offer. They felt that such a clash would be worth ten times the amount offered if it were for Halimi's world crown. Come that eventuality, Gilroy could dictate his own terms: patience was now the name of the game.

McAree was perceptive and knew that Gilroy was by no means the finished article and needed more fights under his belt before a world title could become a reality. In the interim, the prime aim for Belfast promoter George Connell was to secure a European title fight for Gilroy, against Italy's Piero Rollo. This fight was expected to take place in the autumn of 1959. In the meantime, Gilroy returned to the ring on 7 March at the King's Hall, when he met France's Jacques Colomb. The Frenchman, whose best days as a fighter were well behind him, was, nevertheless, confident prior to his clash with Gilroy, laying a £1,000 side bet that he would beat the Irishman.

Meanwhile, John Caldwell had returned to the ring in Glasgow on 5 February on the undercard of a bill which was topped by Frankie Jones, who successfully defended his British flyweight title against fellow Scot Alex Ambrose. Caldwell's ten-round points victory over Frenchman Henri Schmid was indifferent to say the least. Schmid had won only two of his previous twenty fights, but he managed to frustrate Caldwell throughout their bout. The main objective of the fight, from Sam Docherty's perspective, had been to showcase Caldwell as a legitimate challenger to Jones's title.

That did not work out. The *Glasgow Herald* was scathing the following day, stating that Caldwell 'had done nothing to suggest that he was any more than a promising newcomer'. Adding that he 'still had an awful lot to learn', the newspaper noted that his defence had been suspect throughout the contest and that a decent puncher would have punished him severely. Despite his poor form, Caldwell's name was added to George Connell's King's Hall bill the following month. He was matched against a tough Spaniard, Francisco Carreno.

On 7 March, Caldwell and Gilroy proved to be a massive draw in their native city. Twelve thousand turned up to see them in action at the King's Hall. Gilroy was in sparkling form as he handed out an unmerciful pounding to Colomb, who, despite being rated as number six in Europe, was caught easily with a series of punishing combinations. After six rounds, Colomb's corner men decided, wisely, that their man had taken enough punishment, and retired him from the fight. It was win number fifteen for Gilroy, in an unblemished paid career.

That same night, John Caldwell erased the lethargic performance he had put in against Schmid in February by stopping Carreno in the fourth round. Prior to the fight, Sam Docherty had revealed that he had offered the reigning world flyweight champion, Argentina's Pascual Pérez, £10,000 to defend his title against Caldwell in either Belfast or Glasgow. For manager Jack McCusker, this was another example of Docherty overstepping the mark. Caldwell, who would not turn twenty-one until May, had fought professionally on only nine occasions: the Pérez fight was a ludicrous proposition. Docherty had made the offer to Pérez without consulting McCusker, and Pérez's camp turned it down; it was an embarrassing episode for Docherty. Caldwell stayed silent. Jack McCusker took note.

The next outings for Caldwell and Gilroy were to take place the Kelvin Hall on 15 April. Gilroy, newly labelled 'the Belfast Basher' by the Scottish press, was matched with Charles Sylla of Senegal in what was to be his sixth fight under promoter Sam Docherty. Ironically, the bill would feature Johnny Morrisey, who was returning to the ring, having recovered from the broken jaw he had received courtesy of Gilroy's fists seven months previously. Caldwell was given the harder task, in the shape of the cunning Pierre Rossi of France, who had won six consecutive fights in 1958.

For Gilroy, it was a straightforward outing as he knocked out his Senegalese opponent in the second round. Again, it was a mismatch, as Gilroy took his time to seize his opportunity, catching Sylla with a beautiful left uppercut, which ended proceedings halfway through the round. For Caldwell, with less than a month to go before he turned twenty-one and became eligible to box for a title, it was vital to put in an eye-catching display. Unfortunately, what he managed was a deserved but quite unimpressive win. Despite controlling the fight, his punches lacked the power to put the Frenchman away, and he had to endure a standing count in the last round when he was caught by an uppercut and found himself on the canvas.

Freddie Gilroy's unrelenting rise finally caught the eye of Jack Solomons, and he added the Belfast man to the undercard for his London show on 2 June 1959. Now rated as a probable world-title contender, Gilroy's potential was too good to overlook, and Solomons elevated him to chief supporting bout for his annual Epsom Derby eve show at the Wembley Arena. The devastating punching displayed by Gilroy in his demolition of Peter Keenan in January had convinced Solomons that the Belfast boxer had what it took to go all the way.

On 2 June, Gilroy was forced to face a substitute when his original opponent, Mario D'Agata, a former European and world champion, withdrew with an injured hand. At short notice, Solomons secured Al Asuncion, from the Philippines, a lean, tough, durable opponent, as Gilroy's challenger. Asuncion had traded blows with Halimi, losing by a knockout in the fifth round. He had also claimed the scalp of Peter Keenan, whom he had fought in Manila in December 1956, winning by a ninth-round knockout. Asuncion was no pushover, but the fact that Solomons had matched him with Gilroy was a sure sign that he wanted to test Freddie's credentials before he invested serious money in the Belfast fighter.

The Wembley event was a complete sell-out, with ten thousand fans present to witness the British featherweight champion, Bobby Neill, topping the bill against the baby-faced 1956 Olympic flyweight champion, Terry Spinks. There was a distinct Irish flavour to the bill, with Gilroy's stablemate Fred Tiedt seeing off Irish-born Paddy O'Callaghan, while perennial Ulster Hall favourite Paddy Graham was unlucky to lose on points to Len Barrow of Wales. Gilroy's arrival in the ring was greeted by a colossal roar from the Belfast and London-Irish contingent. They knew the fight would be pivotal to Gilroy's career prospects and, with Solomons promising to offer Halimi £7,000 to box Gilroy if he won, it was vital that Freddie delivered.

The fight began slowly, with the boxers measuring each other up. The roars of Irish support soon rolled around the arena, as Gilroy began to show his ruthlessness, catching the Filipino with expert left hooks to the body. Freddie was out-scoring his opponent by three punches to one and was coasting to victory – until the fifth round. Then Asuncion threw a brutal right hook, which brought a gasp from the crowd as Gilroy's legs wobbled. The referee watched Gilroy intently, expecting him to fall to the canvas, but, somehow, he found reserves of strength and reacted with a flurry of defiant punches. The crowd erupted.

Suitably recovered, Gilroy went on to score an impressive points victory, making him the talk of London. For long periods, he bewildered Asuncion with his variety of punches, forcing him to cover up in helpless defence; the right hand to the ribs had drained the power from Asuncion. Gilroy had impressed on the biggest stage in the

British Isles, in front of an appreciative crowd, earning himself a place in the top five of the world's bantamweights. The twenty-three-year-old Belfast man had conquered Belfast, Glasgow and now London.

That night in Belfast, the *Irish News* received more than two thousand phone calls enquiring whether Gilroy had won. The *Daily Express* labelled Gilroy 'a butterfly among bears', while Solomons, when asked about his future plans for Gilroy, said, 'I'll be thinking of nothing else for the next few weeks. This is the first time I have seen Gilroy, and no wonder the crowds loved him. He's got the goods.' Gilroy had truly arrived on the world stage, and Mr Boxing was now the driving force that would guide his career towards further glory. Predictably, with Gilroy now the darling of the London press, the back pages of the tabloids soon stopped referring to him as 'Ireland's greatest prospect', and switched to 'Britain's greatest prospect'.

Caldwell, meanwhile, had turned twenty-one on 7 May, so he was now eligible to fight for a professional title. At the top of the hit parade, the late Buddy Holly stood proudly with 'It Doesn't Matter Anymore'; for Caldwell, that sentiment was curiously true. In his professional career to date he was undefeated, but now he had arrived in the big time, and all that had gone before was merely reputation. He had to win something to prove his credentials, emulate Freddie Gilroy and stake his own claim in the world rankings. With Caldwell now based in Glasgow, the role of Jack McCusker as his manager was waning ever further, as Sam Docherty effectively pulled the strings in his career. Docherty's immediate aim was to secure a match for Caldwell against the reigning British flyweight champion, Frankie Jones, who had claimed the vacant title in 1957 and defended it on only one occasion. He was a durable champion, but, with Caldwell's class to the fore, Jones was living on borrowed time.

Sam Docherty recognised that he possessed pure fistic gold in John Caldwell. He promoted his next fight in Firhill Park on 18 June, a bill topped by the future European lightweight champion, Dave Charnley, who faced Derry's Billy 'Spider' Kelly. Caldwell's opponent, Italy's Giacomo Spano, had failed to win in any of his previous eights contests and was considered to be something of a whipping boy for up-and-coming prospects. (With Caldwell standing on the threshold of a British title, there was no chance he would be pitted against a dangerous opponent.)

In a fight reported as 'monotonous', Caldwell boxed himself to an unimpressive ten-round points victory over Spano. Lacking power in his punches, Caldwell threatened to stop the proceedings only once, when he sent his opponent to the floor with a stinging right hook in the second round. Durable and crafty, the Italian survived to frustrate Caldwell, whose lack of stamina became obvious as the fight progressed. John was never in danger and deserved his win, but questions had been raised about his ability to take Jones's British title in the near term.

For Billy Kelly, it was yet another night of frustration. Having difficulty dealing with Charnley's southpaw stance, Kelly was disqualified in the sixth round for consistently ducking low. The decision by referee Frank Wilson was greeted with dismay by most of the twenty thousand spectators, many of whom had travelled from Derry to see their hero. As the referee left the ring, he was attacked by a Kelly supporter, and ugly scenes followed as police intervened. It was the third such episode of chaos to greet a Kelly defeat and did nothing to enhance the reputation of boxing.

After the summer break, Gilroy's journey towards a European title fight continued, as he was matched again with former world champion Mario D'Agata, at the Wembley Arena on 15 September. The Italian had withdrawn with a hand injury from his original date with Gilroy three months previously. However, still under contract to fight for Jack Solomons, D'Agata agreed to meet the Belfast boxer over ten rounds as chief supporting contest to the British title clash between John 'Cowboy' McCormack and Terry Downes. Also included on the bill were Fred Tiedt and Paddy Graham, as Solomons aimed again to fill the arena with the ever-growing and vociferous band of Irish fans that had been following Gilroy's London career.

The most striking thing about Mario D'Agata, apart from his nickname, Mario the Moody, was that he had been born deaf. Special coloured lights were flashed in the corner of the ring to signal to him that rounds had begun and ended. At thirty-four, he was a veteran whose best days were well behind him. In 1956, he had beaten Robert Cohen in front of thirty-eight thousand fans in Rome to claim the then European-recognised world bantamweight title, only to lose it seven months later to Halimi in Paris.

That fight had been notable both because Halimi had earned France's first world boxing title in over twenty years, and also because of an incident in the third round. As the round progressed, a loud bang had interrupted proceedings, and a portion of the lights above the ring had exploded, showering the boxers and the referee with metal, glass and smouldering rubber. D'Agata received a burn to his back, which was to scar him for life. However, after a fifteen-minute break, the referee deemed it safe enough for the fight to continue, and Halimi duly won on points. Since then, D'Agata had won the European title from Federico Scarponi in 1958, only to lose it subsequently to Piero Rollo. He was not considered to be a real threat to Gilroy.

With twelve thousand spectators packed into the arena, and with a very interested Jack Solomons prominent at ringside, Gilroy knew that he had to impress to secure a crack at Rollo's European crown. D'Agata, despite his advancing years, took the fight to Gilroy, and in the third round he floored the British champion twice with venomous hooks to the body. Gilroy was entering new territory as a professional, with a real battle on his hands against a crafty and powerful opponent. The sixth round was not much better for Gilroy, who was bundled through the ropes by D'Agata after the Italian had opened up with a barrage of punches.

In the eighth, a swift left hand connected with Gilroy's ribs and left him gasping on his knees, enduring a count. Towards the end of the fight, there was additional worry for the Gilroy camp, as D'Agata opened up a gaping cut over Freddie's left eyebrow. Despite the good work of Jackie McHugh in the corner, the wound began to pour blood in the last round. Luckily, the fight was too advanced for the injury to matter. The Belfast boxer had been made to look ordinary and vulnerable by a man who was proving that he was far from finished in boxing circles.

By the end of the fight, however, Gilroy's hand was raised in victory. He was indeed a lucky man and was awarded the win narrowly, having out-boxed D'Agata in six of the ten rounds. In the seventh, ninth and tenth rounds, the Irish contingent had been on its feet as Gilroy threatened to stop the contest with the Italian rocking all over the ring, soaking up fierce body shots. In D'Agata, Gilroy had faced a cagey boxer who had lived up to his reputation as the 'human octopus'. Whilst he had not won in style, Gilroy knew that he had beaten an opponent who was still a top-class fighter.

Using sign language and communicating through his interpreter, D'Agata praised Gilroy, but urged those who wanted the Irishman to fight for a world title in 1959 to be cautious. It had been Gilroy's toughest fight to date, but he had come through on points and now it was up to Solomons to consider whether the British champion was ready to meet Rollo in London for the European title. In Belfast, George Connell waited on Solomons's determination. If Jolly Jack was to lose interest in Gilroy, Connell stood ready to pounce and stage Gilroy vs. Rollo in Belfast, in front of another record crowd.

Although Caldwell was now twenty-one, Frankie Jones's camp was distinctly reluctant to put his British flyweight title on the line.

Technically, a British champion had to defend his title once every six months, but that rule had long been long overlooked by the British Boxing Board. Dave Charnley, who had won the British lightweight title in 1957, would not defend his crown until 1961, while the light-heavyweight belt had remained unclaimed since Randolph Turpin's retirement in September 1958. In May 1959, Jones had fought twice in the space of three weeks, winning narrowly against Glasgow's George McDade and losing in Manchester to Derek Lloyd.

Then Jones contracted jaundice and was forced to take a long lay-off, leaving Caldwell without a credible opponent. With a crack at the British flyweight title now on the long finger, Caldwell's options were limited. The British flyweight division was stale and in dire need of an injection of class to help shake it up. Still managed by Jack McCusker in name only, John's first outing since June was at the King's Hall on 3 October on a George Connell-promoted bill. The fact that Scotland would face Ireland in an international soccer game at Windsor Park that afternoon ensured that the boxing bill would be attended by a bumper crowd.

Caldwell was to top the bill against a tricky Italian with a powerful punch, Salvatore Manca. The Italian was well regarded and had enjoyed an illustrious career as an amateur, losing to Caldwell in Dublin in 1957. Having won eight of his opening nine paid contests, Manca had gone off the boil somewhat and came to the King's Hall having lost against Salvatore Burruni for the Italian flyweight title.

A full house cheered to the rafters as Caldwell entered the ring. What they witnessed, though, was boring in the extreme. It was ten rounds of scrappy, indifferent boxing, which Caldwell won on points. The referee had to intervene constantly, as both boxers got caught up in clinches. The stamping of impatient feet was audible throughout the bout. Although Caldwell won, his reputation suffered at the hands of the crafty spoilsport Manca. In his ringside seat, Sam Docherty watched with frustration. Caldwell needed a test, and

Docherty sought to match him with a stern opponent for his bill in Glasgow on 28 October.

That opponent was, yet again, Salvatore Manca. Docherty had originally secured Finland's European champion, Risto Luukkonen, for a non-title fight. Two days before the bout, though, a telegram arrived at Docherty's Glasgow office, advising that the Finn had damaged a hand in training and was unavailable. With tickets for the fight at a premium, Docherty sought to save his bill by matching Caldwell with the promising Frenchman Albert Younsi. Unfortunately, that plan was scuppered when Younsi opted to box in Paris on 2 November instead.

So it fell to Manca to fill the void, much to the dismay of the travelling Belfast fans. Docherty tried to stimulate interest in the fight by claiming it would be a chance for both boxers to atone for their less-than-inspiring fight in Belfast. As it turned out, the fight was another truly boring encounter, during which Caldwell showed the greater urgency and stopped Manca in six rounds. It was a one-sided contest which was spoiled again by the Italian's wrestling style and Caldwell's inability to land a telling punch. Now with fourteen victories under his belt, Caldwell needed something special to spark his career back to life.

With the European Boxing Union recognising Gilroy as the number-one challenger for Rollo's crown, the fight was put out for purse offers; the deadline was 26 October. George Connell, still counting the profits from the Gilroy vs. Keenan encounter in January, was determined to secure the fight for Belfast. He offered the champion £4,000 to come to the King's Hall in early December. Standing in Connell's way was the matter of Rollo's title defence against Federico Scarponi on 3 October. Rollo's management assured Connell that, if successful, the Italian would come to Belfast to fight Gilroy.

Connell rubbed his hands with glee when Rollo retained his title after Scarponi was disqualified for headbutting. The promoter was certain that the attendance record at the south Belfast venue would be tested as he pencilled in 5 December for the fight. That was, until Jack Solomons re-entered the fray and decided that he wanted to promote the fight in London. In the background, Jolly Jack had already done a deal with Rollo and had secured his signature to fight Gilroy in London. The contest was set for Wembley Arena on Tuesday, 3 November 1959. Connell, not surprisingly, was fuming.

Rated at number five in the world, Piero Rollo came to London to face Gilroy that evening with a record of fifty-five fights and only five losses. Aged thirty-two and noted for having an appearance akin to that of a film star, Rollo had won the Italian title in 1957 and the European crown a year later, which he had defended twice thereafter. Solomons promoted the fight as an eliminator for Joe Becerra's world title. Regardless of the outcome, Solomons boasted to the press, on the morning after the fight, that both Gilroy and Rollo would be in his office awaiting a phone call from Los Angeles, which would confirm which one of them had won a tilt at Becerra's world title.

Speaking to Left Lead in the *Irish News*, Solomons was emphatic regarding his future plans for Gilroy. 'I fully expect Freddie to beat Rollo,' he said. Adding, 'If he does, I will move the Himalayas, if necessary, to bring Joe Becerra from Mexico to London to defend his world title in the New Year.' For Gilroy, the Rollo fight was now a make-or-break affair. In Belfast, anticipation was at fever pitch, with over a thousand fans having booked accommodation in London for the occasion. Gilroy and McAree were forced to train in Newry, forty miles outside Belfast, to escape the hype and the adulation of the Belfast fans. Eventually, Gilroy's training regime, thanks to extensive sparring with Jimmy Carson, who had fought Rollo in 1957, was completed and, suitably fit and confident, he travelled to London for his date with the champion.

The presence of large Belfast and London-Irish contingents in the arena made for a truly raucous occasion. For those who couldn't be there in person, legendary commentator Eamonn Andrews kept millions of fans abreast of the proceedings live on BBC radio. The top of the bill that evening saw John 'Cowboy' McCormack lose a thrilling battle with Terry Downes for the British middleweight title. It was, however, Gilroy who stole the show, with an assured performance over fifteen rounds to outpoint Rollo.

Entering the ring to a fanfare of trumpets, Gilroy was a clear winner, with eleven of the fifteen rounds being awarded to him. His body punches beat a resounding tattoo off Rollo's ribs, while sustained hooks kept the Italian on the back foot throughout the contest. Only once did Rollo threaten to upset Freddie's battle plan, when he landed a hard right hand in the seventh round that shook the British champion. Undeterred, Gilroy bounced back with enthusiasm and coasted home through the last five rounds to win, and ignite scenes of Irish joy in the packed hall.

In Ardoyne's Northwick Drive, Freddie's sister, Emily, screamed the good news up the stairs to a praying Mrs Gilroy. The crowds danced in the streets, but the now-traditional bonfire would not be lit until the hero returned the following evening. In London, Freddie was hoisted high by Jackie McHugh and Jimmy McAree. He had become the first British or Irish boxer to claim a European title since Belfast's John Kelly had taken Peter Keenan's title from him at the King's Hall in 1954.

In his dressing room, he was handed a telegram of congratulations on behalf of the Prime Minister of Northern Ireland, Sir Basil Brooke. Others followed from Belfast's Lord Mayor, Alderman Robin Kinahan, sports stars, personalities and hundreds of well-wishers from Britain and Ireland. To round off what had been an epic week and year, within days of the fight, Gilroy was named the British boxer of the year by the Boxing Writers' Association.

The following morning, however, Jack Solomons did not receive a phone call from the world champion's handlers. Solomons's plan to match Gilroy with Becerra was dealt a critical blow when America's National Boxing Association (NBA) determined that Becerra was to defend his world title against Halimi in February 1960. For a supremely confident Gilroy, with three titles to his name, patience was now the name of the game. It was estimated that his crack at the title would not come until the autumn of 1960. That would allow Gilroy time to build up the additional experience which many observers felt he needed before taking on the ultimate challenge.

Accordingly, Gilroy accepted a lucrative offer – said to be in the region of £1,000 – to defend his Empire title in December in Belfast on a bill promoted jointly by Solomons and Connell. His opponent, Bernie Taylor, the South African bantamweight champion, was an unknown quantity, with just eight fights under his belt. As Gilroy entered the ring in Belfast, he was afforded a rapturous ovation by the crowd of fourteen thousand. He sent the tall Taylor to the canvas within two minutes. In the fifth round, three crushing hooks sent Taylor's gum-shield flying and, within seconds, he was sprawled on the floor, gasping for air. It was over. Gilroy had won his nineteenth fight, without breaking a sweat. The crowd applauded the brave South African, but it was Gilroy's night and, as 1959 ended, he was standing at the pinnacle of his career.

At the end of December, the NBA announced its world rankings. In the bantamweight division, Gilroy was ranked as the number-two contender, behind Halimi and the champion, Becerra. Caldwell, without a title to his name and still five months short of his twenty-second birthday, was considered the number-four contender to fly-weight champion Pascual Pérez's crown. In an era when there were only ten world titles, Irish boxing had never had it so good. Two box-ers from the terraced streets of Belfast had battled their way almost to the pinnacle of the hardest sport in the world, without defeat and without fuss. It was an incredible statement of their boxing ability, and Belfast and Ireland were truly honoured. In 1959, fate had been good to Freddie Gilroy and John Caldwell. What could possibly go wrong?

10.

DOCHERTY CASTS HIS SPELL

With Freddie Gilroy standing on the cusp of a money-spinning world-title shot, it was natural that promoter Jack Solomons would also begin to take a keen interest in the thriving career of John Caldwell, the second of Belfast's Terrible Twins. Docherty could not match Solomons for money or influence in world-boxing terms, and Solomons was the man who could bring Caldwell's career to the next level. That, though, would upset the apple cart. If Caldwell were to come under Solomons's wing, Docherty would become surplus to requirements. Manager McCusker held a seven-year contract to manage Caldwell's affairs, whilst Docherty, the man who had pro-moted the Belfast man's career to date, held no legal claim on the boxer.

With John now moving swiftly up the word rankings – towards serious money – the future management of his career would become a battle between McCusker and Docherty. It was a battle that had been brewing for some time: McCusker had been unhappy about the growing relationship between Docherty and his boxer. The farce in Glasgow in October, which had led to Caldwell fighting Salvatore

Manca for the second time within a month, had left McCusker angry, but isolated. At stake was a point of principle as to who ultimately had the final say over the direction of the flyweight's career.

By early December 1959, the beginnings of the final split between Caldwell and McCusker began to surface. In the seven weeks since the victory over Manca, McCusker had not heard from either Caldwell, who was training in Glasgow, or Docherty. McCusker had been frozen out, and he wanted the situation resolved before he lost his protégé completely. Docherty, like McCusker before him, had become almost a surrogate father to Caldwell. He had given Caldwell employment as a clerk in one of his bookmakers' shops, helped him find a house in Lennoxtown outside Glasgow, provided him with a car, and showered him with money and gifts. He had convinced John – with nods, winks and promises of riches – that he would make him a world champion. At merely twenty-one, the Belfast boy had been caught in Docherty's spell.

In early December, Solomons held talks with McCusker in Belfast and returned to London with a two-fight deal for Caldwell. First, it would see him make his London debut on 12 January on a Stan Baker-promoted bill at the Streatham Ice Rink. His opponent would be the former European champion, Young Martin. Second, should Caldwell impress Solomons sufficiently, would be a non-title bout with the reigning European flyweight champion, Risto Luukkonen, at the Wembley Arena in late February. If all went to plan, Caldwell, within the space of two months, would go from relative obscurity to red-hot boxing property. Should that happen, Caldwell, McCusker and Solomons all stood to gain financially; Sam Docherty did not.

In Scotland, Caldwell had joined the Dalmarnock Road gym run by Docherty's sidekick, Joe Aitcheson, who, although a Scot, had previously trained the Royal Ulster Constabulary's boxing team. Caldwell sparred with top-class opponents, such as Billy Rafferty, Derry Treanor and Bobby Neill. He had no need to train in Belfast –

much to McCusker's acute frustration. In desperation, McCusker sent a letter by recorded delivery to Caldwell in Glasgow, asking him to contact him as a 'matter of urgency'. He received no response. With the dispute festering, Docherty, who knew that he could muster – and pay for – the legal arsenal required to wrest control of Caldwell from McCusker, was typically outspoken in his views on the rift. 'Caldwell is my responsibility and will fight only when I order him to. I intend to seen this thing through to the bitter end. I have taken legal advice on the matter and hope to have my position clarified as soon as possible,' he stated.

Caldwell was content that his career was moving in the right direction under Docherty and Aitcheson. 'I was happy, and attended Mass at half six every morning,' he recalled. 'After that, I would take to the hills for running and stamina training.' In addition, an invitation to train with Belfast's Charlie Tully and the Glasgow Celtic team was to good an offer to pass up.

> My exercise routines came under the notice of the then Celtic manager Jimmy McGrory, who asked me to help the team out. I took the players for physical workouts to help them get fitter, and we all became very friendly . . . I remember those training games, and none of the Celtic players were not allowed to tackle me as I was in training for fights, so it was a strange experience to be able to run rings around my heroes.

Under Aitcheson, Caldwell's training regime was second to none. Joe knew Caldwell inside out and was a motivator as well as a strict disciplinarian. 'Joe could tell exactly what stage I was at during my training and how I was shaping up in the run-up to a bout,' recalled John. 'He always cautioned me against being overly fit, and he sensed just by my mood when I had reached perfect fitness; that was when I lost my temper in the gym. At that stage, it was a case of no more physical work, as he was sure I was ready.'

Back in Belfast, Jack McCusker's influence was waning further. Jack was a very humble, good-natured, working-class man, who was fighting a losing battle against a man of Docherty's capacity. Jack was suffering also from the early stages of throat cancer, and the prospective break-up of his relationship with Caldwell was not conducive to his health. McCusker possessed a legal contract binding Caldwell to him, but the boxer was determined to make a break from his Belfast manager. The situation was a mess, and McCusker felt compelled to act.

In late December, McCusker wrote to the British Boxing Board to make a formal complaint concerning Docherty's involvement with Caldwell. Tellingly, he named his boxer as a willing accomplice in the affair. 'My conscience is clear,' Jack wrote. 'After all, it was Docherty who asked me to manage Caldwell.' Both Caldwell and Docherty were summoned to appear in front of the Board at its meeting on 6 January 1960, but they failed to turn up, claiming that they had 'not been given sufficient time to prepare a defence'.

The Board suspended Docherty's promoter's licence, indicating that he would remain suspended until he appeared in front of them in person. It was a stalemate. The megaphone diplomacy continued in the sports pages. It was a public-relations disaster. Caldwell withdrew from his 12 January fight with Young Martin, claiming to be suffering from pleurisy. He threatened to move to the United States to continue his career, a move which would have invalidated his contract with McCusker. He then went public, offering McCusker £2,000 to release him from his contract. McCusker was not impressed. 'I've handled John Caldwell since he was ten years old, and taught him all he knows. I am not interested in selling his contract. I believe I can take him to the world title,' he said.

Stan Baker rescheduled Caldwell's fight with Young Martin for 9 February. McCusker claimed he had negotiated John a fee of £500 to appear, and said that fee was 'an amount far in excess of what Caldwell had ever received for boxing in Glasgow under Docherty'.

The impasse persisted, but Caldwell agreed to take the fight, insisting that McCusker would not be in his corner on the night. It was an assertion McCusker was happy to contradict. 'I feel it is my duty to look after John's interests. I'll be there,' he said. On the day of the fight, McCusker left for London with the sole intention of being in Caldwell's corner, but Caldwell threatened to leave the ring if McCusker tried to take his place in the corner. McCusker's complaint against Docherty and Caldwell was due to be heard formally by the British Boxing Board in London the following day.

The weigh-in for the fight took place that lunchtime at Streatham Ice Rink. An uneasy peace prevailed as McCusker watched from afar. Caldwell tipped the scales at 8st 2lb, while Martin weighed in two ounces lighter. As the crowd filed into the south London venue, the talk was as much of the drama which might ensue in Caldwell's corner as of the fight itself. McCusker blinked first. With a public bust-up a distinct possibility, he decided to appoint Nat Sellers, who had been corner man for the late Freddie Mills, as his replacement. Also overseeing Caldwell would be Aitcheson. For McCusker, an embarrassing place among the press was as close as he got to the proceedings.

The bookmakers were predicting a first defeat for Caldwell. Martin was twenty-eight years old and had won the European title four times. The first came with a knockout victory over Cardiff's Dai Dower in Nottingham in 1955. That encounter had been notable because Martin had floored Dower on thirteen occasions. Known as 'the Spanish Tornado', Martin, a former jockey, had lost most of the fire of his early career, but he still posed a serious threat to Caldwell's unbeaten record.

Despite the shenanigans outside the ring, Caldwell put on a display that was cool, calculated and defiant. Left Lead, in the *Irish News,* considered it 'a massacre', as the Spaniard was knocked out cold with ten seconds of the third round remaining. 'He [Caldwell] needed no referee, just twin referees of his own – one in his left fist and one in his right,' added the *Irish News*'s correspondent. The medics immediately rushed to the helpless Martin. It took more than two minutes for him to rise gingerly to his feet and make his way to his corner.

From Caldwell, Aitcheson and Sellars, there was no elation, just an acceptance that it had been a job well done, despite the difficult circumstances. It was an ice-cool demolition job, which answered a lot of critics who had dared to doubt the Cold-Eyed Killer. Without fuss or frills, Caldwell left the arena and returned immediately to Glasgow; he had no intention of appearing before the British Boxing Board the following day, nor had Sam Docherty.

Jack McCusker remained in London to put his case to the Board. Representing Caldwell at the meeting was the Glasgow solicitor J. P. Murphy, who requested that the hearing be adjourned until March, since Caldwell had returned to Glasgow to prepare for his 23 February fight with Risto Luukkonen. The solicitor argued that, by insisting that Caldwell appear, the Board would be interfering with his fight preparations and, by extension, his career. The officials accepted the argument and adjourned the hearing for a second time, pencilling in 9 March as the new date. It was another small victory for the Caldwell-Docherty camp, and a sign that the boxing officials were, perhaps, not treating McCusker's grievance with the gravity it deserved. McCusker did not object and returned to Belfast, while Caldwell's preparations for the Luukkonen fight continued in Glasgow. It seemed that the longer the Board procrastinated, the less clout McCusker's complaint had; inertia suited Caldwell and Docherty.

John remained in Glasgow ahead of his debut under Solomons. His non-title fight against Luukkonen, the reigning European champion, was to be the main supporting bout to Dave Charnley's clash with Sauveur Benamou of Algeria. Charnley, a firm favourite with the London crowd, was making his return to the ring after his bid for the world lightweight title against Joe Brown had ended with a cut eye in November 1959. Docherty was still suspended and Caldwell again refused to have McCusker in his corner; he was again to be mentored at ringside by Joe Aitcheson and Nat Sellers.

As before, McCusker travelled to London for the fight. The animosity was apparent at the weigh-in: neither boxer nor manager spoke. As the fight neared, McCusker, much to his – and Caldwell's – embarrassment, again took a seat among the press. The prize for Caldwell, in theory, should he beat Luukkonen, was spelt out by Jack Solomons in his programme notes. 'If John Caldwell, the Pride of Ulster, can beat Finland's Risto Luukkonen, then there will be real Jack Solomons dough on the line for a return fight – with Luukkonen's European title at stake.' Yet again, Caldwell's career was at a junction, with Solomons watching as a very interested spectator.

At twenty-nine, Luukkonen was a worthy European champion and possessed boyish good looks that he had maintained through skilful defensive boxing and a counter-punching style. He had only fought professionally on twelve occasions, but had won all save one of these contests, drawing the other. His style was awkward, prancing around the ring, waiting for opportunities to score points. Caldwell was supremely fit and, as he entered the ring for his fifteenth paid fight, many pundits felt that his precocious talent would see him home. Indeed, he forced the pace from the beginning and was an easy winner on points.

To observers at ringside, Caldwell's performance had been far from world-beating, though. Peter Wilson of the *Daily Mirror* noted that Luukkonen 'must surely have been the poorest European champion at any weight to have ever appeared in a British ring'. Only once had Caldwell been in trouble, when, in the sixth round, on being told to break, he had dropped his hands and taken a clean right hook to the jaw. Luckily, the Finn's punch lacked any serious power, and the fight went to its mundane end in front of an eerily silent crowd. Though unimpressive, the win proved that Caldwell would not be troubled in taking the European crown. At the end of the month, the NBA rated Caldwell at number eight in its world rankings; not bad for a man without a title – or a manager.

Despite Caldwell's victory over Luukkonen, the Finn agreed to defend his European title against Spain's Young Martin. Caldwell, who had defeated both men, was decidedly upset by this turn of events. The British title was still there for the winning, though. In late February, promoter George Connell sent a telegram to Joe Gans, manager of British champion Frankie Jones. The message was simple and to the point: 'Jones title bout – offer date 23 April. Reply very urgent.' The response from Gans was short: 'Regret Jones not fit for April.' Jones knew his time as champion was coming to an end. The British Boxing Board had agreed to permit him one more defence of his title prior to any clash with Caldwell, and Jones wanted to make as much money as possible before the inevitable occurred. The British title fight between Caldwell and Jones was postponed until the autumn.

On 9 March, the Board met and determined that the complaint by McCusker against Caldwell and Docherty was a matter for those three to resolve among themselves. With a family and a house to keep, Caldwell needed money and he needed to box. So, as an interim measure, Solomons matched him with George Bowes, whom Gilroy had beaten in 1958, for 29 March at Wembley Arena. Caldwell accepted the fight, but McCusker refused to allow his boxer to appear. With the wrangling ongoing regarding his contract, in the week before the contest, Caldwell received a legal writ threatening legal action if he went ahead with the fight. Two days before the bout, Caldwell called Solomons and advised him that he could not box Bowes. Peter Wilson of the *Daily Mirror*, who seemed to act as a one-man appreciation society for Solomons, started referring to John as the 'problem child' of British boxing. Wilson was happy to relate how John had reversed the call charges to Solomons, something which had greatly upset the 'rotund impresario'. In the end, Belfast's Peter Sharpe filled in for Caldwell against Bowes, losing a close ten-round contest.

With options limited in Britain, Solomons looked towards Europe and the United States for opponents for Caldwell. Jolly Jack's annual promotion at the Wembley Arena on the eve of the Epsom Derby was part of the London sporting calendar and was always a house-filler. Topping the bill on 31 May would be Dave Charnley, who would face the Californian Paul Armstead in a ten-round international contest. Caldwell's name was added to the undercard when he was matched with France's flyweight champion, René Libeer. The Frenchman had previous knowledge of Caldwell, having shared the rostrum with him in Melbourne, where they had both claimed bronze medals. He arrived in London with an impressive sixteen successive victories under his belt.

The dispute between Caldwell and McCusker remained unresolved. With Jack undergoing major throat surgery and Docherty still suspended, Caldwell was essentially managing and supervising his own affairs in Glasgow. For roadwork, he chose the picturesque Campsie Fells in Glasgow's northern suburbs, where the great Benny Lynch had trained a generation previously. It was a messy state of affairs for the Irishman as he prepared for his third London appearance. He was on his own.

The fight itself was inconclusive. With Joe Aitcheson and Nat Sellers again in his corner, Caldwell was awarded the narrowest of victories on points, but his inexperience had been witnessed by the large London audience. At least half the crowd in attendance had booed when referee Joe Hart raised John's hand at the end of the fight. He had lacked power behind his punches in a contest that was fast but uninspiring. The outing had done nothing to underline any notions that he was ready for the world title. With his seventeenth win under his belt, and no immediate crack at the European or world title in the offing, Caldwell focused on the long-awaited fight with Frankie Jones.

George Connell eventually secured Jones's signature to defend his title against Caldwell in the King's Hall on Saturday, 8 October. Jones had not defended the title since February 1959 and was installed as a complete underdog. The interest in the fight in Belfast was phenomenal, with a seating plan for the arena drawn up to accommodate at least seventeen thousand fans. Barry McGuigan, when he defended his world title against Bernard Taylor in September 1985, fought in front of eight thousand, which was considered the maximum the King's Hall could accommodate. To double that figure presented a logistical nightmare in stewarding and safety terms, and the potential for disaster was ever-present. Yet the Belfast public rolled up in their thousands to buy tickets, and more than a thousand fans came over from Glasgow.

The day of the fight coincided with the Ireland vs. England Home International at Belfast's Windsor Park. However, Desmond Hackett of the *Daily Express* wrote that he was more interested in seeing Caldwell, 'the man with eyes greyer than a Belfast sky', claim his first title. Jones was known as 'the Solemn-Faced One' and came to Belfast with the intention of defending his title successfully and, therefore, winning a outright Lonsdale Belt outright. Caldwell had remained in Glasgow under the eye of Joe Aitcheson. He was described in the *Glasgow Herald* as being 'pale and drawn' as he left for Belfast prior to the fight. Such was the confidence of Sam Docherty – who, still suspended by the British Boxing Board, was now describing himself as Caldwell's 'official adviser' – that he had booked himself a flight to Los Angeles to secure a world-title deal for John with Pone Kingpetch.

The day started badly in Belfast for locals, as England, thanks to two goals by Jimmy Greaves, saw off Northern Ireland by five goals to two. The assembled crowd in the King's Hall then witnessed

Jimmy McAree's other protégé, Fred Tiedt, lose to Sandy Manuel with a cut eye, while Jim Jordan lost on points to the Scot Alex McMillan in a lightweight contest. Despite these setbacks, the King's Hall crowd erupted as Caldwell made his walk to the ring. Sporting a tight crew cut, he looked fit and determined as the bell rang to signal the start of what would be one of Caldwell's finest displays. McCusker was conspicuously absent.

On Monday, the *Irish News* reported Caldwell's display in the following terms:

> What a marvellous battering Caldwell gave Jones before knocking him cold in the third round with a crunching right to the jaw which dropped him flat on his face in a muddled, motionless heap. That final blow had followed another one which had sent the champion tottering back. The end in a way was merciful. This was the keyed-up killer Caldwell – the most impressive display I have ever seen him give. I know that Jones was a softer touch than I honestly expected, but how efficiently he [Caldwell] carried out his task.

Seven minutes and twenty-two seconds of total superiority had won Caldwell possession of a Lonsdale Belt. The final, telling onslaught had been clinical in the extreme. John's coup de grâce had been delivered with assurance and, with pity and compassion, his gloved hands supported Jones to the canvas to meet his fate. The *Daily Mirror* commented that Jones was counted out as he lay motionless on the floor but 'at seven he twitched slightly, like a dog asleep in front of the fire'. In the dressing room, Jones announced his retirement from the sport.

For Caldwell, the roars of approval were singular confirmation that the future was bright, and potentially brilliant. As the massive crowds flooded onto the Lisburn Road, George Connell and Sam Docherty were busy trying to agree on a lucrative figure to offer Pone Kingpetch for a money-spinning clash in either Belfast or

Glasgow. However, the man who really had the sway – and, indeed, the money – to secure such a fight was Jack Solomons, who had watched the Caldwell-Jones fight with interest from ringside. Docherty's offer to Kingpetch was turned down, and Caldwell agreed to appear again at the King's Hall on 26 November. He stopped his opponent, former French champion Christian Marchand, in the seventh round.

Three days before his fight with Marchand, Caldwell had announced that Jack McCusker had agreed to release him from his contract. With the prospect of a costly court battle in the offing, McCusker had realised that he was fighting a losing battle and had agreed to accept an undisclosed amount from Caldwell as compensation. 'I'm happy that our differences have been settled,' John told the press. 'Jack's a great guy and a great trainer, and I wish him a speedy recovery to health. We will always be firm friends.' A successful relationship, which had begun in 1950, was now at an end; McCusker was ill and his inner fight had been sapped completely. Within days, Docherty announced that he had applied for a manager's licence.

11.

ZURDO PINA SPOILS THE PARTY

Glasgow's Billy Rafferty was nominated to fight Freddie Gilroy at the King's Hall on 19 March 1960, in a fight which would see the Clouting Cherub's three titles on the line. Rafferty was a tough character whose grandfather hailed from Belfast. With no amateur record of note, he had taken up boxing in his late teens and had fought twenty-five times, losing four times and drawing once. In Glasgow, he had joined up with Joe Aitcheson, and it was then that his fortunes in the ring had begun to change for the better. Under Aitcheson, Rafferty's style had changed in the ring, and he came to the King's Hall with six successive wins under his belt.

Although Rafferty had recorded only one knockout, he had sparred extensively with Caldwell in Glasgow and felt that he held the key to unlocking Gilroy's defence. 'I will chase Gilroy from the first bell until I am lying flat on the floor with the referee counting to ten over me – or until I am standing triumphant in the ring with that glittering Lonsdale Belt around my waist,' Rafferty told Belfast's *Northern Whig*. Unwisely, Rafferty added that he had a 'secret weapon' – he was going to box as a southpaw, instead of in his usual orthodox style. McAree and Gilroy noted this tactical indiscretion; Rafferty had given away the element of surprise.

On the morning of the George Connell-promoted bill, Jack Solomons arrived in Belfast promising the earth, the moon and the stars to Freddie Gilroy, should he beat Rafferty. A contract to fight Joe Becerra at Wembley on 31 May was the prize on offer, according to Solomons. Should that fall through, Solomons added, 'I've plans too for a special titbit for Irish fans – Gilroy and John Caldwell in Belfast, possibly in the open air.' It was evident that Solomons knew where the money lay and was plotting the most lucrative career path for Gilroy, Caldwell and, most importantly, himself.

The King's Hall was jammed with fifteen thousand fans expecting Gilroy to win with ease. That seemed the likely outcome when, in the first round, Gilroy landed a clean left hand to Rafferty's chest, which winded him and sent him to the canvas. Referee Jack Hart administered a count of eight, but Rafferty survived amid the deafening noise. The Scot then put up a game challenge, but he was finding Gilroy's southpaw style troublesome.

In the seventh, Freddie opened up a cut over Rafferty's eye. Gilroy stood off his opponent, picking his shots and, by the thirteenth round, Rafferty's eyes were pouring with blood. The referee stepped in, stared at Rafferty's eyebrows, and stopped the fight. Gilroy had successfully defended his three titles and was edging closer to a world-title crack. Afterwards, Rafferty, who required three stitches over his eye and had to have his ear drained of blood, described Gilroy as the 'hardest hitter I have ever met'. Trainer Joe Aitcheson said of the stoppage, 'You can get another fight, but not another eye.'

It was now up to Jack Solomons to decide whether he would pull out the stops to get Gilroy his promised world title; he had, of course, some sums to do. On the flight back to London after Gilroy's win, Solomons leaned over in his seat and told the *Daily Mirror*'s Peter Wilson, 'If we can't get the world-title fight for him [Gilroy] at

Wembley on 26 April, he could fight Johnny Caldwell in the open air in Ireland and draw a crowd of fifty thousand.' Regardless of Gilroy's world-title ambitions, Jack Solomons, two and a half years before they met in the ring, knew exactly how much the clash of the Belfast Terriers was worth.

In the 1960s, Harry 'the Horse' Levine was, in boxing terms, the greatest rival to Jack Solomons when it came to fight promotion. The British fight scene was not big enough for two egotistical Jewish pro-moters, and the rivalry festered until the men detested the very sight of each other. Levine had originally worked under Jolly Jack, but had branched out when he realised he could make just as much money promoting bills through the extensive contacts he had established.

Levine had been watching Gilroy's progress under Solomons with keen interest. In early April 1960, he spotted an opportunity to mus-cle in on the Belfast champion's career. With Becerra under contract to box Kenji Yonekura in Tokyo in May of that year, Gilroy had little prospect of a crack at the world title until the autumn. With many in the boxing fraternity of the view that Gilroy needed a further warm-up fight before he was ready for Becerra, Levine offered Gilroy what seemed to be a straightforward outing against twenty-five-year-old Mexican Ignacio 'Zurdo' Pina in Manchester on Monday, 25 April.

Based in California, Pina was managed by the flamboyant Liverpool-born Russian Jew Harry Kabakoff. Pina and Kabakoff had arrived in London for the Gilroy contest talking up the prospect of an upset, pointing out that Becerra had turned down $25,000 to meet Pina in a non-title fight. The moustachioed Pina, who had pre-viously served an apprenticeship as a bullfighter, exuded confidence as he spoke to the media through his interpreter, sporting a som-brero and prominent gold teeth. Kabakoff turned a few heads – and stomachs – when he described his boxer's pre-fight diet. 'Raw liver and raw eggs, mixed with honey and tequila: that's where he gets his strength,' he said.

With a record of twenty contests since 1957, there was nothing on paper to suggest that Zurdo would trouble Gilroy, who had accepted £1,100 to take the fight. Such was the Belfast man's pre-fight confidence that he took no time off from his day job in Beltex. Jimmy McAree advised Left Lead in the *Irish News*, 'Raw-meat eater or not, we're not underestimating Pina – Gilroy has the beating of him.' In boxing, however, the most dangerous opponent is the one you know little or nothing about.

Harry Levine, who had promoted the fight as a final eliminator for the world title, was happy to tell reporters that he had Becerra lined up for the winner of the contest. As Gilroy's spies watched Pina spar in London, they noted that his right-handed stance seemed somewhat awkward and his punches appeared to lack power. Zurdo had perhaps overstated his case when he had predicted an upset.

Events, though, began to work against Gilroy. His preparations took a turn for the worse on the day before the fight when his entourage, which included fellow Belfast boxer Jim Jordan, missed their flight from Belfast to Manchester due to car trouble. This caused panic. The problem was eventually resolved when seats were secured on a flight to Glasgow, with a late connecting flight to Manchester. It was the type of hassle that Gilroy did not need going into a fight against an opponent he had somewhat underestimated.

The following evening, the crowds poured in to see Ireland and Britain's most talked-about boxer in Manchester's Belle Vue. As the bell rang for the first round, Pina came out fighting with an orthodox style, which is what Gilroy expected. With a minute to go in the round, though, he suddenly switched to southpaw, completely throwing Gilroy's tactics off course. It was a master stroke. Gilroy had fallen for the oldest boxing trick in the book.

Pina was a natural left-hander and had completely fooled not only Freddie and his entourage, but the press and spectators too. Zurdo, Pina's nickname, was also a Spanish word meaning 'left-handed' or 'lefty', but no one in Freddie's camp sussed that before the fight. Within seconds, Gilroy was caught flush on the chin with a right hand and went down for a count of five. A potential disaster was at hand for the Belfast boy. He fought back gamely, only to find himself being out-boxed by an opponent who had most certainly done his homework.

Pina knew every skill in the boxing trade and expended every ounce of sweat and ring-craft to steer clear of Gilroy's rushing tactics. He peppered Freddie's face with a constant left hand and countered with skilful, well-aimed punches. Three times during the fight, he made Gilroy look like a novice by feinting out of reach, leaving his opponent floundering over the ropes. Gilroy was untidy as he chased Pina, looking for a knockout punch. He was merely playing into the hands of his opponent, who boxed with calmness and refused to enter into a brawl.

With two rounds to go, Freddie, in his twenty-second fight, was staring a first defeat squarely in the face. He was also on the verge of losing any legitimate claim to a crack at Becerra's title. The last six minutes were crucial. While Gilroy did catch his opponent, Pina refused to go down; he held on to claim the victory. It was a disaster for Gilroy. The decision was booed by a large section of the crowd but, on leaving the ring, Pina was afforded a standing ovation. He had won fairly, and the boxing aficionados appreciated that fact.

Gilroy's dressing room was a depressing place in the aftermath of the defeat. Freddie shed painful tears, but nobody knew what to say. He had been outfoxed and out-boxed by a crafty opponent, and his career prospects had been severely damaged. 'We can't grouse,' said Jimmy McAree. 'All I can say is that a sharp Gilroy would have beaten him. Yes, we were a trifle put out by the upsets in our travel, but I am not offering that as an excuse.'

Pina's manager knew that his boxer had pulled off a massive upset and had fooled Gilroy. 'We had a surprise plan – and it worked,' said

Kabakoff. 'We don't know whether Gilroy had ever fought a south-paw. But we guessed that he had never fought one as good as Pina.' In winning, Pina had staked a claim to meet fellow-countryman Becerra for the title. He had proved his class against Gilroy, whose defensive limitations had been emphatically exposed.

No bonfires greeted Gilroy's arrival in Belfast the following evening. McAree told the press that there were 'niggling' issues he would address in the following days regarding Freddie's style. He blamed Gilroy's use of his new car for his lack of sharpness and promised to take away his keys in the run-up to his next fight. He blamed the botched travelling arrangements. Mostly he blamed him-self for not making sure his boxer took the fight seriously enough. That night, Freddie spent a number of hours under surveillance in the Royal Victoria Hospital while specialists carried out tests on a damaged eye socket. It was an anxious time for Gilroy. Speaking to Left Lead of the *Irish News* regarding the immediate plans for Gilroy, McAree was diplomatically evasive. The correspondent noted, 'Wild horses would not have dragged those plans out of Jimmy McAree.'

Amid the diminished glory of Gilroy's boxing career, prepara-tions for his marriage to his long-standing fiancée, Kay Martin, at the end of May continued. Despite the defeat, being a triple cham-pion brought its own accolades and novelty outings. Take, for exam-ple, 2 May 1960, when Gilroy appeared at Arsenal's Highbury Stadium in the annual Sportsman's Aid Society football match, which set the boxing and horse-racing fraternities on one side, against a show-business eleven on the other. Lining up at outside left in front of a crowd of twenty-five thousand in North London was a young Gilroy, alongside Henry Cooper and Dave Charnley.

Facing the pugilists and jockeys was a side including Sean Connery, fresh from starring in *Darby O'Gill and the Little People*, Tommy Steele, Des O'Connor and the legendary former England captain Billy Wright. It was an occasion that must have left the young

Ardoyne boxer somewhat star-struck. The roars and laughter of the Highbury crowd, though, could not dampen the deep pain that the defeat to Pina had caused Gilroy.

In late May, Freddie Gilroy and Kay Martin were married by Father Timothy O'Regan in Ardoyne's Holy Cross church. His best man was his brother Teddy; his sister, Emily Kelly, was the matron of honour. Hundreds of well-wishers lined the Crumlin Road to cheer the couple as they left for a honeymoon in County Kerry. In the Gap of Dunloe, the couple were feted in a local pub, where the patrons partook of the local 'friendly' custom of punching the champion in the stomach. Thankfully, tradition precluded Freddie from retaliating.

12.

ROBBERY AT THE WEMBLEY ARENA

As bantamweight champion of the world, Joe Becerra had the world at his feet. He was, however, a haunted man. The ghost who haunted him was a Texan by the name of Walt Ingram, who had died after a non-title fight with Becerra in October 1959. Ingram, brave to the end, had been subjected to a ferocious onslaught from the champion. At the start of the ninth round, Ingram's manager, Mike Davis, fearful for his fighter's health, tried to persuade his boxer to retire in his corner. Ingram, somewhat disorientated, claimed he was not hurt and insisted that he be allowed to continue.

It was a fatal act of bravado. In the ninth round, the punishment continued, forcing the referee to intervene with a minute to go. Ingram collapsed soon afterwards and was admitted to hospital in a comatose state. He died six hours later, leaving behind a wife and three children. Becerra was devastated. He had remained at the hospital throughout Ingram's ordeal, praying for his opponent. When all hope seemed lost, he broke down in great distress. From that moment onwards, Becerra, formerly known as the Brave Little Bull, lost much of the fire and conviction that had made him a star.

Becerra had claimed the world crown in early 1959, when he

Caldwell (left) and Gilroy in May 1956, while in Chicago
for the Irish Golden Gloves tour

Caldwell (left) with trainer Jack McCusker and Willie Green in 1954

Caldwell made his mark by beating Chris Rafter in front of a packed Ulster Hall on 17 April 1956, securing a place on the Irish team bound for the USA.

Captain T. D. Morrison of the Ulster Boxing Council wishing Caldwell, Gilroy
and Martin Smith well on their trip to the Olympics, 12 November 1956

Gilroy with his Irish Amateur Boxer of the Year Award in 1955
Photo courtesy of Ardoyne Pics

Caldwell cools off after training, Glasgow 1958
Photo courtesy of the Caldwell family

Gilroy with his Lonsdale Belt, after defeating Peter Keenan, January 1959
Photo copyright © *Belfast Telegraph*

Promoter 'Jolly Jack' Solomons, pictured here in February 1959, soon realised just how lucrative both Caldwell and Gilroy would become.

Gilroy's first defeat, to Ignacio 'Zurdo' Pina in May 1960

Gilroy shows off his Lonsdale Belt to boxing fan
Peter Thompson in June 1960. The belt is missing.

Gilroy catches Alphonse Halimi, at Wembley Arena in October 1960.
'That defeat really bugged me,' Gilroy recalled later.
Photo courtesy of Brian Madden

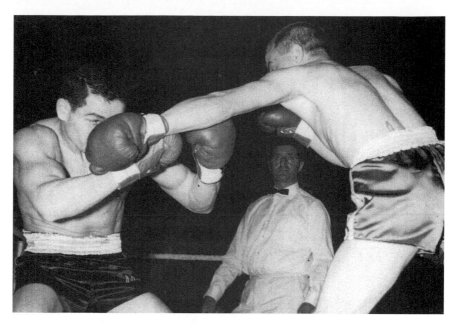

Le Petite Terreur, Halimi (left), fights Caldwell in 1960. The French-Algerian was to box both Gilroy and Caldwell for world titles in the space of seven months.
Photo courtesy of the Caldwell family

Caldwell, the bantamweight world champion, shows off his trophy in May 1961. He beat Halimi at Wembley Arena to win the title.

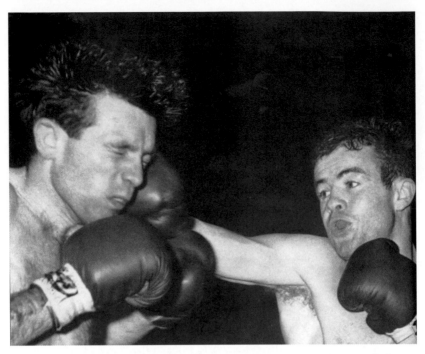

Gilroy catches Billy Rafferty with a right in a March 1962 fight
that saw Gilroy claim a Lonsdale Belt outright.
Photo copyright © *Belfast Telegraph*.

Éder Jofre stalks Caldwell in São Paulo, in January 1962. With 18,000 fans
screaming 'Kill him!' Caldwell was lucky to get out of Brazil in one piece.

Gilroy (left) and Caldwell (right) sign the contracts in May 1962 to fight each other at the King's Hall that October, as (left to right) Jimmy McAree, Jack Solomons, George Connell and Sam Docherty look on.

GEORGE CONNELL

AND

JACK SOLOMONS

PRESENT

International Boxing

Featuring the British and Empire Bantamweight Championship

FREDDIE GILROY   v   JOHN CALDWELL

KING'S HALL, BALMORAL

SATURDAY, 20th OCTOBER, 1962

A programme for the King's Hall clash

Gilroy (left) tries to comfort Caldwell (seated),
who has just lost their October 1962 King's Hall clash.
Photo copyright © Mirrorpix

Gilroy with his Texaco Hall of Fame Award in 2005
Photo courtesy of Belfast Media Group

An ill Caldwell (left) with Brian Magee, Holy Trinity Gym, Belfast, 2006
Photo courtesy of Belfast City Council

Ten-year-old Liam Neeson pictured with his hero,
Gilroy, in North Street, Belfast, 1962

Gilroy is reunited with Neeson after forty-eight years,
on 5 September 2010, at Belfast City Hall.
Photo copyright © The Belfast Boxing Ring

In 2010, Gilroy and Neeson recreate their 1962 photograph at Belfast City Hall.
Photo copyright © *Daily Mirror*

defeated Halimi in Los Angeles with an eighth-round knockout. He had gone on to defend that title twice, stopping Halimi in a rematch and shading a decision over Kenji Yonekura in Tokyo in May 1960. In August 1960, Becerra fought two further non-title fights. He knocked out Chuy Rodriguez in his first outing. Then, three weeks later, fellow Mexican Eloy Sanchez stopped Becerra in the eighth round of their fight in Ciudad Juarez.

Becerra retired immediately after the Sanchez fight; he could not shake off the ghost of Walt Ingram. It was a shock to the boxing world, and it set in motion a split within America's National Boxing Association (NBA), as a squabble to appoint a new champion developed.

To work out the complications in the NBA that led to both Freddie Gilroy and John Caldwell fighting for a version of the world bantamweight crown in the space of seven months is complicated, to say the least. Boxing has historically been littered with more fights, bust-ups and squabbles outside the ring than inside it. By the start of the 1960s, the NBA, which, in partnership with the European Boxing Union and the British Boxing Board, effectively ran world boxing, had lost its credibility. Boxing was under severe public scrutiny, as deaths, rumours of thrown fights and betting coups, and claims that the organisation was controlled by the Mafia, undermined the body.

In January 1960, the members of the Californian Boxing Commission resigned in protest at the NBA's apparent lack of will to rid the sport of its shadier elements. Soon, the New Jersey and Massachusetts bodies followed suit. In April 1960, Nat Fleischer, the doyen of boxing journalists and founder of the hugely successful magazine *The Ring*, criticised the NBA, accusing it of indifference to the 'hoodlum influence'. All this ultimately split the organisation, leading to two versions of the world bantamweight title being fought for between October 1960 and January 1962. None of this helped to improve the sport's image in the public eye.

While it had seemed certain, prior to his defeat by Pina, that Gilroy would be matched with Becerra for the world title, fate was playing its hand in the background. Within weeks of Becerra's abrupt retirement, what remained of the NBA matched Éder Jofre of Brazil with Sanchez, who had conquered Becerra, to fight for the vacant title in Los Angeles in November 1960. While Sanchez was considered a classy fighter and held the Mexican title, his elevation to world contender was a complete surprise. The Mexican had beaten the world champion, but that had been in a non-title fight, and he was not even listed among *The Ring's* top ten bantamweights for 1959. *The Ring* had named Halimi and Gilroy as the number-one and number-two contenders – and Jofre as the number-four contender. The European and British branches of the NBA were understandably upset that the Americans had overlooked Halimi and Gilroy.

Given the NBA's loss of credibility, Jack Solomons saw a chance to assert his prominence in world boxing. The British and European contingents of the NBA were not prepared to accept the snub from their American counterparts. Solomons seized his chance and made arrangements to host his own European version of the world bantamweight title. On 19 September, a deal was struck between Halimi's handlers and Solomons for Halimi to meet Gilroy over fifteen rounds at 8st 6lb for the vacant 'world title' on Tuesday 25 October at the Wembley Arena in London.

The British Boxing Board and the European Boxing Union both recognised the fight as a world-title contest, despite the Americans laying claim to their own version. In a statement, the president of the British Boxing Board, Mr J. Onslow-Fane, said, 'We are not prepared to accept the arbitrary decision of the NBA of America, made without consulting any other controlling body, that Éder Jofre will meet Eloy Sanchez for the vacant title.' As number-one contender in *The Ring's* ratings, Halimi could justly claim that the option to fight Gilroy gave him the right to assert a claim to the world crown. As holder of the British, Empire and European titles, Gilroy's credentials were obvious. Solomons's move was bold, and he pointed out that, if there were two 'world champions' at bantamweight, it would be no different to the situation which existed at middleweight.

After losing to Pina, Gilroy had taken time out from boxing to reassess his career. Holidaying in Niagara Falls, though, an incident occurred which convinced him that his future lay in boxing. One afternoon, Freddie and his wife Kay were walking through the resort when the screams of a woman alerted them to a mugging. Armed with a knife and in possession of the woman's bag, the robber made his escape – until he came into contact with Gilroy's famed left hook. Lying unconscious, face down in the street, the robber was duly arrested. The Belfast man had been the hero, and the incident satisfied him that his punching power remained intact.

Gilroy's hunger for boxing was reborn, but there was a problem. Since the Pina fight, Gilroy's appetite had been insatiable. Chocolate, ice cream and fish and chips – all washed down with sugary soft drinks – had added to his girth. He was two stones overweight by September 1960. It would be hard for him to make the weight for the Halimi fight. Rumours of Gilroy's weight problem soon came to the attention of the press. In early October, the *Daily Express* put into print its fears about Gilroy. CHOCOLATE KID MUST SLIM DOWN was the headline over an article by Sydney Hulls, which suggested that Gilroy was on his way to heavyweight rather than bantamweight if he did not cut out the fatty foods. The message hit home for the Gilroy camp. A regime of salads, sparring and tedious roadwork was the only solution.

Alphonse Halimi was a class act. Known as La Petite Terreur ('the Little Terror'), Halimi was extremely proud of his Jewish roots, and his shorts were adorned with the Star of David. Raised in a family of sixteen in Algiers, Alphonse was a child tailor before he was adopted by a well-to-do French widow named Marcelle Faty. He held the undisputed bantamweight crown from April 1957, when he beat Mario D'Agata on points in Paris, until July 1959, when he was knocked out in the eighth round of his clash with Joe Becerra in Los Angeles. During that time, he had not defended his crown, but had instead embarked on a lucrative exhibition tour, which had netted him almost £60,000.

One such exhibition bout against Belfast's Jimmy Carson at the Harringay Arena in June 1957 had ended in a notable defeat for the French-Algerian. Beforehand, the press had labelled the contest a 'mismatch' and an 'act of butchery', criticising Solomons for even contemplating putting Carson into the ring with Halimi. But with Halimi putting in what was described as a 'lamentable performance', Carson had effectively out-boxed the champion. By the ninth round, Halimi had sustained a cut eye, which forced the referee to stop the fight. It was an embarrassing defeat; along with two defeats to Becerra, this was the only blotch on Halimi's record.

Accordingly, Gilroy sparred long, hard rounds with Carson in preparation for his own Halimi fight. He knew that he stood on the cusp of a world title, even if it was a disputed crown. The excess weight came off, and the Gilroy team headed to London high in confidence. GILROY CAN PUT BRITAIN BACK ON THE WORLD TITLE BANDWAGON, announced the headline for the *Boxing News*'s upbeat preview of the fight. It tipped the Belfast man to become the first British or Irish fighter to win a world title since Randolph Turpin held the middleweight crown for sixty-four days in 1951. Leaving Belfast that morning to cheer on Gilroy was another former world champion, Rinty Monaghan, who entertained the large Belfast contingent with his songs and stories.

By the time Gilroy entered the ring to a hero's welcome, over ten thousand spectators had packed into Wembley Arena to make it a truly special occasion. The arena had been taken over by the Irish and the atmosphere bordered on the frenzied. Belfast came to a standstill to listen to live radio coverage of the fight. The boxers touched gloves and returned to their respective corners for the most eagerly anticipated fight of 1960. Promoter Jack Solomons was a very satisfied man.

Gilroy dominated the fight from the start. He peppered Halimi with hard body shots. The pace of the contest was almost reckless, with Gilroy, if anything, showing too much eagerness. The Frenchman tied up Gilroy countless times in clinches, spoiling any strategy the Belfast fighter tried to impose. It was a case of the bolder Gilroy throwing caution to the wind as he went in search of the telling shot that would wound his prey. By the third round, Gilroy's lack of caution was punished as he shipped a stinging left hand from the Frenchman.

Gilroy refused to yield, but Halimi's spoiling tactics made the contest an ugly affair, with referee Philipe de Backer being forced to shout 'break' on thirty-nine occasions. By round seven, Halimi knew he was in trouble and upped the pace. He caught Gilroy with a sweet hook, but the blow only served to provoke the Irishman into a spirited rally, which had the crowd on its feet. The Irish contingent could almost taste a historic win; their man was, without doubt, in front.

Gilroy's extreme fitness was apparent for all to see. He chased his opponent around the ring, landing punches with precision. For Halimi, the bout was reaching crisis point as round thirteen arrived. It would take something special to turn the tables. This duly arrived. The Frenchman started the round with purpose, and his uppercut was beginning to pose a real danger to Gilroy. With fifteen seconds left in the round, Gilroy charged at Halimi and was caught with the sweetest of right hands, which sent him crashing face-first to the canvas, inches from his corner.

Jimmy McAree's heart missed several beats. Defeat was seconds away for Gilroy. *Boxing News* noted that Halimi had landed a 'perfect punch' and described the moment: 'Oh, how that hushed the crowd!

You could almost hear Halimi's heart pound with excitement.' Gilroy looked anxiously at his corner as the referee's count reached four. Time was running out; he was hurt. Five, six. Then an unmistakable, piercing sound interrupted the tragedy. Gilroy had been saved by the bell.

Freddie was noticeably groggy as he slumped onto his stool. For McAree, the next sixty seconds would be the most important of his boxing life. He urged Gilroy back to his senses. The fight was back in the balance. Time raced for the Gilroy corner and round fourteen began as the bell rang out. It was a subdued Gilroy who left his stool and touched gloves with a rejuvenated Halimi. The Frenchman could sense that his chance had arrived, and he wobbled Gilroy with neat hooks. Gilroy battled on gamely, but it was an excruciating round for the Irish contingent; their man was hanging on for dear life.

Gilroy had come into the fight at 8st 4lb, two pounds under the agreed limit. Every last ounce he had shed was now costing him dearly, as his stamina wilted. Seconds now lasted minutes, while the crowd shouted encouragement. Gilroy's only tactic was to hold on and frustrate Halimi. The bell finally sounded and, again, it was in the hands of McAree to inspire his protégé to victory. The crowd was at fever pitch as the last three minutes of action began. Gilroy stood on the threshold of greatness, while Halimi was one perfect punch away from the title.

The boxers touched gloves for a final time, and the Belfast fighter surged forward. He was operating on pure adrenalin as the crowd stood to roar him home. Halimi had momentarily lost the upper hand, and the roof of the venue was being tested as the noise again reached a crescendo. After the agony of round thirteen, a Gilroy win was back within reach. All he had to do was hang in there. The Frenchman seemed to be a spent force. Amazingly, with seconds left, Gilroy had Halimi trapped in a corner and was dishing out a tremendous milling. Amid the chaos, the final bell sounded to signal the end of the epic battle. The boxers embraced as the referee approached them to declare the winner. Irish eyes would not be smiling for long.

Halimi's arm was hoisted within the brilliant light of the ring. It was a stunning defeat and was greeted by uproar in the arena. Froth-filled beer cans landed on the canvas as boos, hisses and catcalls rang out. '"Mercy upon us, ye robber!" shouted a man as big as Finn McCool at the referee,' began the Press Association's somewhat stage-Irish report. The police were called to avert a riot, and eventually calm was restored. How a battle-happy Belfast crowd would have reacted to such a decision at the King's Hall would have been violently predictable.

Amid the anarchy in the ring, Gilroy shrugged his gallant shoulders in sad acceptance. Halimi, who seemed to be genuinely surprised at the verdict, sportingly embraced Gilroy, who was still coming to terms with the shock of what he felt had been a diabolical decision. Halimi then turned to a French television cameraman and shouted dramatically, 'I have avenged Joan of Arc!' The Frenchman had forgotten, obviously, that he had beaten an Irishman and not an Englishman. The celebrations of the French fans echoed around Wembley Arena as the Irish contingent filed out into the dark London night in disgust. Eventually, Freddie made his sad, subdued departure from the ring and headed for his dressing room. The inquest began. Bitter tears were merely minutes away. The post-mortem was going to be hard medicine for Freddie.

In the hidden depths of the arena, the Halimi dressing room echoed with jubilant cheers; three doors away, the silence in Gilroy's was ghostly. Eventually, the large body of journalists was admitted to interview Gilroy, and the quotes were gathered for the morning papers. Gilroy spoke softly, almost in a whisper, saying that he thought that he had been a clear winner. 'I forced the pace throughout; that knockdown must have given him the edge,' he said. Asked if he would have beaten the count in round thirteen without the help of the bell, Gilroy responded, 'Definitely. I signalled to my corner that I was OK. It was a good punch, but it certainly would have not kept me down for the full count.' Halimi's version of the fight was, not surprisingly, at odds with Gilroy's; he considered himself a worthy winner. After receiving stitches in a cut eye, the Frenchman walked to Gilroy's dressing room and embraced his opponent warmly. 'Gilroy was a strong fighter, very courageous; he was a gentleman in the ring and gave me a very hard fight,' Halimi said.

Freddie Gilroy avoided the subdued post-fight party in his hotel that evening to go to his room and try to sleep away the pain. At the top of the charts stood Roy Orbison, with 'Only the Lonely'. How apt that title was for Gilroy that night. Halimi was champion and nothing would change that fact. Yet the Frenchman knew that that he had been in a war, one from which he had been lucky to escape with the crown. *The Ring* was to vote the contest the third-best of 1960, but that was scant consolation for Gilroy. For Jack Solomons, a rematch was needed – urgently – to rectify what he labelled 'the injustice' of the decision; he said he would pay Halimi twice the purse the boxer had earned for the Wembley battle. Apart from Halimi, Solomons had been the winner.

In their considered reports, the press, far away from the catcalls and cries of 'daylight robbery' in the arena, were quite circumspect about the outcome, with most having Gilroy half a point in front at the final bell. Joe Bromley of *Sporting Life* saw the knockdown in round thirteen as crucial in swaying the decision in Halimi's favour. Desmond Hackett, in the *Daily Express*, thought the battling last round by Gilroy should have swung the decision in the Belfast man's favour. Crucially, referee de Backer went public to reveal that, in fact, Gilroy had been beaten on his scorecard by the very narrowest margin and his trip to the canvas had been the deciding factor. His scoring had been seventy to sixty-nine in the Frenchman's favour, with the referee adjudging Halimi's technique to have been more effective than Gilroy's force and attack. De Backer added:

> rounds thirteen and fourteen were vital to the result, and the champion won both by clear margins. Even if the last round had been Gilroy's, the pair would have been equal on points at the end, and I'd still have given Halimi the decision as the better of two fine craftsmen.

The two points gained by Halimi in round thirteen for the knockdown had effectively swayed the decision.

To this day, Teddy Gilroy, Freddie's brother, is convinced that the referee made a monumental error after the fight. He explained:

> There had been a row before the fight when it was found out that Freddie was to wear black shorts with a red trim, which were exactly the same ad Halimi's. Both had crew cut haircuts and it was impossible to tell them apart – the referee was confused at the end and chose the wrong hand.

Freddie too was certain the referee got it badly wrong in the Wembley Arena that night. In his recollection:

> I had out-boxed Halimi throughout the fight and I was sure that I had won . . . The two of us were in the corner shaking hands at the final bell when the referee came over and raised Halimi's hand and I am sure in all the confusion he had awarded the fight to Halimi by mistake. By that stage it was too late to change the decision; it was my second professional defeat and it really, really bugged me.

Indeed, the Halimi defeat was hard medicine for Gilroy. Nevertheless, there was always a chance to redeem himself in the rematch. Or so Freddie had been told.

13.

HAMMERED IN BRUSSELS

Good news arrived for both Freddie Gilroy and John Caldwell at the end of January 1961. *The Ring* rated both Belfast men as second in the world rankings in their respective divisions. Despite this, Gilroy's confidence was at a low ebb, and Solomons was procrastinating on naming a date for a rematch with Halimi.

Freddie's bantamweight ambitions were slow to reignite after his shuddering defeat to Halimi. Indeed, his progress towards a promised rematch with the champion was slow, and anything but impressive. On 31 January, both he and Caldwell appeared on a bill at the Royal Albert Hall. Labelled again by the London press as Belfast's Terrible Twins, they enjoyed victories in front of the packed hall, but it was evident that all was not well in the Gilroy camp.

Having not trained for two months in the aftermath of his defeat by Halimi, Gilroy's four-week preparation for the fight with the Italian Ugo Milan had been interrupted by a bout of severe influenza. The issue of Gilroy's weight again became a factor and, when it became obvious that he would not make the agreed 8st 9lb for the fight, it was deemed a catch-weight contest at 8st 12lbs. At the

weigh-in, Gilroy was twelve ounces inside the new limit, but noticeably a full five pounds heavier than his opponent.

The theory that Gilroy was not at his tip-top best proved to be well-
founded when the Irishman walked into a venomous right hand from
the Italian in the first round and was sent crashing to the canvas.
Although he got to his feet before the referee had reached two in his
count, a frantic Jimmy McAree ordered the boxer to take a neutral corner to receive the full eight-count. Composure now was everything.
The Italian moved in frantically to finish off Gilroy, who shipped a
serious barrage of punches. Yet Freddie composed himself as the
round progressed and, eventually, despite lacking any real punching
power, boxed his way to an easy victory on points over ten rounds.

John Caldwell's fight with Angelo Rampin was stopped in the
eighth round when the referee intervened to save the Italian. It was,
however, a lacklustre performance by the British champion against
an opponent with limited boxing ability. Although Caldwell made
heavy weather of the fight, a final onslaught of punches forced the
referee to act. The crowd was less than charmed by the performance,
and boos rang out in the hall as Caldwell preserved his unbeaten
record. Solomons, though, was a contented man as the two Belfast
men had won, and his hand was strengthened as negotiations continued for world title-fights for them.

While the world bantamweight division was in disarray, the flyweight class was far more straightforward. In April 1960 in Bangkok,
Pone Kingpetch of Thailand took the title with a split decision over
the Argentinean incumbent, Pascual Pérez. At twenty-five, the Thai
boxer, who had been a Buddhist monk, became a legend in his country and seemed destined to hold the title for a prolonged period. In
a rematch five months later at the Olympic Stadium in Los Angeles,
Kingpetch stopped the Argentinian to retain the title. Solomons
began negotiating a crack at the title for Caldwell, who was setting
the pace in Europe.

On 1 March, Solomons announced that he had matched Caldwell with Kingpetch, with a June date in Dublin pencilled in for the clash. The only outstanding difficulties remained money, and the insistence of Kingpetch's management that three neutral judges and a neutral referee be appointed to oversee the proceedings. 'I think I can get over these difficulties and I have given an assurance to Kingpetch that Caldwell, if he wins, would defend the title in Bangkok,' stated Solomons. Predictably, however, negotiations soon stalled, and the fight was put on hold. In reality, Kingpetch would not countenance coming to Ireland to defend his crown.

Meanwhile, with his options limited, Sam Docherty was thinking three moves ahead. He knew Solomons had earned big money by creating a European version of the world bantamweight title. With Gilroy and Halimi due to meet in a rematch, Solomons had created a veritable cash cow. Docherty wanted in on the action. Caldwell was the key, and Docherty made it known that his boxer was considering a move up to bantamweight. He threw down challenges to both Gilroy and Halimi to meet Caldwell.

One view is that this was, from Docherty, impertinent, to say the least. The other view is that Docherty was being shrewd and hedging his bets that Caldwell could mix it with the best in the higher division. A match with the flyweight champion from Thailand was seen as too costly and risky; pragmatism was the order of the day. Peter Wilson of the *Daily Mirror*, commenting on Docherty's assertion that a bout between Caldwell and Gilroy in Belfast would 'go down very well', wryly pointed out that, 'Having experienced some rather hectic nights in Belfast, I reckon a Caldwell vs. Gilroy fight wouldn't be the only thing that would go down there!'

In early March 1961, Terry Leigh-Lye of the *Irish Times* visited a smiling, wisecracking Gilroy at the St John Bosco gym, where he found the Belfast boxer to be back to his fighting best. Gilroy reported that the extraction of three teeth the previous week had 'done him the world of good', and he was now even enjoying his gruelling roadwork for the first time in years. Jimmy McAree told Leigh-Lye that Gilroy's doctor had told him that a gum infection had meant that Gilroy had been swallowing poison, which had been the root cause of his lack of fitness. With the extraction of the teeth, Gilroy's manager was certain that the fighter would return to full fitness. However, since his defeat to Halimi, Gilroy's fondness for chips, chocolate and sugary drinks had made a noticeable effect on his torso.

In mid-March, Caldwell disposed of Jacques Jacob in five rounds at the Colston Hall in Bristol. The fight was a complete mismatch, with the Frenchman having won only five of his thirteen professional contests. The following evening at The Stadium in Liverpool, Gilroy's rehabilitation in the bantamweight ranks continued, with a comfortable victory over Billy Calvert. The bout was a catch-weight contest fought at 8st 12lbs, a full six pounds over the bantamweight limit. Gilroy was never troubled by the Sheffield boxer, who was merely a journeyman and took severe punishment as the Belfast man's power and ring-craft dictated matters. Three weeks later, Gilroy knocked out Edinburgh's Jackie Brown in the fourth round of their clash at Paisley Ice Rink. The *Glasgow Herald* reported that the end of the contest came 'inevitably and with stark suddenness', as Gilroy felled the Scot with a right to the solar plexus. The Belfast man was again beginning to assert himself with gusto in the ring, and the date for the rematch with Halimi was now only a matter for Jack Solomons to determine.

At the end of April, Gilroy made a successful reappearance at Belfast's King's Hall, stopping Algeria's Boualem Belouard in seven rounds. The Algerian, with a record of four defeats in eight professional contests, was yet another lamb to the slaughter for a resurgent Gilroy, who boxed at half pace and looked noticeably drawn, having come down to 8st 7lb for the contest. It was, though, a job done without fuss, and it was apparent that Gilroy was back in contention for a crack at Halimi's title. His next fight on that road was scheduled for 27 May against Pierre Cossemyns in Brussels, for the Belgian's European bantamweight title. It looked like a straightforward match for Gilroy, who had defeated the Belgian with ease at the King's Hall in 1958.

However, as Gilroy set his sights on a Halimi rematch in September, it seemed that, for Jack Solomons and Sam Docherty at least, there was an alternative plan afoot. Gilroy was struggling with his weight and, by now, realistically, should have moved up to featherweight. He was losing a battle to make the bantamweight limit and seemed weaker the closer he came to it. A piece of boxing skulduggery was about to shatter his world-title dream.

By late April, with the world flyweight clash between Caldwell and Kingpetch seemingly dead in the water, the boxing fraternity was rocked when Solomons announced that he had matched Caldwell with Halimi for the world bantamweight crown at Wembley Arena on 30 May. For Solomons, Gilroy was not ready for a rematch with Halimi. He pointed out that, if Caldwell were to beat Halimi, Gilroy would be matched with Caldwell for the crown.

'This is one fight where I can forget about a profit,' said Solomons. 'I won't be able to afford the matches to light my Coronas, but that doesn't worry me in the least.' Such assertions by the promoter were, as usual, treated with scepticism. The news was greeted in the Gilroy camp with shock and anger. Solomons had given Gilroy a tremendous slap in the face. For manager Jimmy McAree, it was an outrage. 'This is a ridiculous match,' said McAree. 'Gilroy is a logical contender for a crack at the title and we will lodge a protest with the British Boxing Board.'

There was every reason for Gilroy's camp to be annoyed. Gilroy had spent four years rising through the ranks of the bantamweight division but now, in his first fight at that weight, John Caldwell stood on the threshold of world glory. The promises by Solomons to Gilroy for an immediate rematch after the Halimi fight had been hollow. It was a case of 'business is business' for the promoter. Amid the criticism, Solomons wrote to McAree to explain his decision.

'I see, according to the papers, that both you and Freddie are upset that Caldwell is to fight Halimi for the world title,' he wrote. 'I sincerely trust that this is just publicity on your part and that you are not really serious.' Going on to explain that the fight made sense for all concerned, Solomons added, 'Should Caldwell win, then it [a Gilroy-Caldwell world-title fight] would be a "natural" for Belfast. He pointed out that if Halimi won, a rematch with Gilroy was a distinct probability. In other words, Solomons was a winner whatever the outcome.

With hindsight, the bitterness between John and Freddie can be traced back to that decision taken by Solomons. Caldwell had taken what Gilroy had felt was rightly his – a promised fight with Halimi. Many observers felt, though, that although Solomons's decision had been cruel to Gilroy, Caldwell deserved the chance. With an unde-feated twenty-one-fight record, he had shown enough class to war-rant his chance at a higher weight. He had youth and freshness and, most importantly, he had been thriving while Gilroy had suffered a loss in form. Caldwell was the boxer in the ascendant and, logically, a better bet to beat Halimi. Solomons knew this. For Gilroy, it was scant consolation that he would fight for a European title three days prior to Caldwell's world-title bout.

With the Caldwell-Gilroy rivalry intensifying, an invitation in early May from the Caldwell camp for Gilroy to spar in Glasgow was turned down. Caldwell would have benefitted greatly, as Gilroy knew Halimi inside out. However, the anger lingered that Caldwell had taken on a fight which Jimmy McAree felt should have been Gilroy's. The Ardoyne man chose to finalise his preparations in Cushendun, County Antrim. For Gilroy, it was a case of knuckling down and accepting the fact that Caldwell had secured the crack at Halimi. The jolt he had received when Caldwell was matched against Halimi seemed to spur him on in his training ahead of the clash with Cossemyns. A win in Brussels would place Gilroy as the main contender against either Caldwell or Halimi for a world-title shot. A defeat in Brussels was unthinkable.

Many observers had noted that Gilroy had seemed to lack power and speed in his three previous fights, but he began to impress in training and was a mere half a pound over the bantamweight limit when he left Belfast for Brussels. McAree expressed satisfaction with the training regime and predicted that his boxer's strength would not be affected, even though he had shed more than four pounds. After all, Gilroy had easily disposed of Cossemyns in March 1958 at the King's Hall and was six years younger than his Belgian opponent. It seemed to be a straightforward assignment for the Belfast man.

The problem was that Cossemyns, despite a mediocre start to his career, had matured as a fighter. One of his most notable victories had been in Belfast in April 1954 against John Kelly, a contest that effectively finished Kelly's top-class career. For five years, Cossemyns was a complete journeyman, recording the aforementioned loss to Gilroy in 1958 during his spiral down the European rankings. In February 1959, Halimi had knocked him to the canvas four times on his way to a third-round stoppage. A month later, he lost on points to the highly rated Londoner Terry Spinks; Cossemyns had knocked Spinks down three times in the fifth round, but had seemed incapable of finishing him off.

That defeat, however, was a turning point for the Belgian, who, thereafter, enjoyed eleven victories, his only defeat coming on points against Gracieux Lamperti during a fight for the European featherweight title. It was noted that the Belgian had developed a crisp right hand, which would pose difficulties for Gilroy, but, at thirty, the press felt he was a fading champion. Cossemyns was upbeat ahead of the fight, claiming that his defeat to Gilroy in Belfast in 1958 had been down to the fact that he was unaware that the Belfast man was a southpaw. Despite that poor excuse, the Belgian would go into the fight as the underdog.

GILROY WILL REGAIN EUROPEAN TITLE, read the headline of *Boxing News* on 19 May 1961. Confidence was high in British and Irish boxing circles. Gilroy's preparations were secretive, but McAree was sure his boxer was ready. Gilroy had been accompanied by his wife, Kay, to the Belgian capital. They relaxed pre-fight with a sight-seeing bus tour. It was left to Kay to pass on snippets about her husband's frame of mind, telling the press, tongue in cheek, that she was sure that Cossemyns would win the fight.

Ominously, the referee chosen for the bout was Philipe de Backer, who had given Halimi the victory over Gilroy seven months earlier. The setting for the fight would be the impressive fifteen-thousand-seat Palais des Sports in the heart of the city. On the eve of the fight, the Harlem Globetrotters had thrilled a capacity audience. On the morning of Saturday, 27 May, the ring was erected for what was to be one of Gilroy's sternest tests. With Caldwell now within a week of his moment of destiny, Gilroy had no margin for error in Brussels.

The fight was a disaster for Gilroy. It soon became evident that he had lost too much weight and was decidedly weak. By the ninth round, Gilroy was a rag doll at the hands of the Belgian, and McAree threw in the towel to end the embarrassment. Cossemyns had, by all accounts, learned from his trip to Belfast in 1958 and punished all of Gilroy's errors. Gilroy's tendency to drop his right hand and to try to battle his way out of difficulty cost him the fight. In the fourth round, he was twice forced to take standing counts when Cossemyns crashed right hands into his face. It was the eighth round, however, which almost settled matters in favour of the Belgian.

Five times during the round, Gilroy was punched to the canvas, as he endured an unmerciful battering. The bell saved him as he tried to get up for the fifth time, but the referee mistakenly signalled that the fight was over, an error which sparked pandemonium in the arena. The referee tried to tell the Belgian that there had been a mistake and the round, not the fight, had ended. McAree was incandescent, almost ready to resume his own boxing career to send the Belgian back to his corner. With a semblance of calm restored, alas, the bell rang out again to signal the start of the ninth, and Gilroy was again hammered to the ground. This time Jimmy McAree could only throw in the towel.

Gilroy was battered and embarrassed. Having won the first three rounds easily, he had begun to showboat, and paid heavily for his arrogance. McAree was shell-shocked by the result. 'He took too many chances when he was ahead on points,' noted Gilroy's manager. 'When he hit the floor for the first time in the eighth round, his head hit the canvas and that did the damage.'

The fight had proved a number of facts about Gilroy's limitations as a boxer. Firstly, his weight problems were now becoming a crucial factor, leaving him weak as a bantamweight. Coming onto the scales at one and a half pounds below the 8st 6lb limit had left him feeble; he had lost too much weight, too soon. Add to that his apparent inability to take a punch, and his future in the world bantamweight division was in tatters. Essentially, the fight had been swung in the Belgian's favour by a left hook he had thrown in the eighth, which, Gilroy conceded, 'Everyone saw coming, except me.'

Gilroy wrote candidly about his future the following Monday in the *Belfast News Letter*.

> This morning I have to make a desperate decision: shall I stay in professional boxing? . . . On Saturday night, instead of being flat on my back, I should have been dancing on the tips of my toes . . . Now, after making a reasonable amount of money and enjoyment, I am wondering after this defeat whether I may now have to say goodbye to professional boxing.

The fight with Cossemyns had been traumatic in many ways for Gilroy, and his battering forced him to enter a period of contemplation. His mind was tortured by the nightmare of Brussels. With three defeats in the space of a year, Gilroy's confidence was at its lowest ebb. His fellow Belfast man, John Caldwell, would enter the ring on 30 May to try to take the world title of the man Gilroy felt certain that he should be fighting. It was hard medicine for Gilroy and there was a distinct possibility that, given Freddie's run of poor luck, Caldwell would be world champion by Wednesday morning, adding insult to injury. One thing, however, was keeping Gilroy ambitious and sane – the defence of his British title. He still dreamt of becoming the first Irishman to win outright the coveted Lonsdale Belt. But this was scant consolation at the end of a disastrous week.

14.

JOHN CALDWELL, WORLD CHAMPION

Prior to his fight with Alphonse Halimi, John Caldwell was visited in his new Hillhead Avenue home in Belfast by Donald Gomery of the *Daily Express*. Whilst still preparing for his fights solely in Glasgow, Docherty and Caldwell had reached an agreement that John would return to Belfast to visit his family between training sessions. Showing off his new house in the suburbs of the city, John was relaxed as he fed chocolate drops to his son John, while his wife, Bridie, dutifully served tea and cakes. In his article, Gomery told the story of a private man who was devoted to his family and to his Catholic faith.

Now the proud owner of an £1,800 house, bought outright through his earnings from professional boxing, John considered himself to have made a comfortable living as a boxer, but not to have become rich. 'A man could put down roots here,' he told Gomery as he surveyed the distant and picturesque Black Mountain overlooking west Belfast. With earning power of £12,000 to £15,000 a year, he yearned for the day when he could finally hang up his gloves, open a business and live like any other family man.

'I have to fight and need to be ruthless in the ring to make a living,' he said. 'Before a big fight,' he added, 'I would go to church and pray for myself – and for my opponent. I pray that he will not be seriously injured, and then I go into the ring and try and hurt him as much as I can.' Touching the bridge of his nose, where his eyebrows met, John pointed out that he had the features of a man who possessed a bad temper. 'I may be ruthless and I do have a bad temper – they're right!' he said. 'But my aim in the ring is to hit my opponent three times for every punch he lands on me – it's as easy as that!'

Fame had come at a price for the bantamweight. Each time he visited his mother's terraced home in Cyprus Street, crowds of admirers and well-wishers gathered around the house, hoping to glimpse Belfast's newest superstar. Men of a more forceful nature sought to prove their street-fighting credentials against the small man they saw as fair game. There is a name in Belfast for such characters – 'slabbers' – and John related how his little hands had been deployed to put manners on those who had been brave enough to challenge him or, as on one occasion, had pulled a bottle on him.

On leaving, Gomery shook Caldwell's tiny hand and noted that, in other circumstances, it was a hand that could lay him on the flat of his back. However, the most striking aspect of the man known as the Cold-Eyed Killer was that, although he was a gentleman outside the ring, he had got where he was in boxing through sheer ruthlessness inside it.

There is an old adage in boxing which says that 'a good big 'un will always beat a good little 'un'. Many pundits were predicting that the heavier and more experienced Halimi would overcome his Irish opponent. They were discounting the fact that Caldwell was at the peak of his career as his chance of a lifetime with Halimi approached. Adding four pounds to his physique gave Caldwell added strength, and the confidence to mix it with Halimi. However, most importantly, he feared nobody. Caldwell had assumed two nicknames from the British press since he had cut his teeth in the flyweight division. Initially, he had been labelled the Baby-Faced Assassin, which was soon followed by his more familiar boxing name, the Cold-Eyed Killer. The latter moniker referred to his greyish eyes, which pierced through a lifeless face of stone. Halimi was about to meet a Cold-Eyed Killer at the top of his game.

The press, however, was quite reserved about Caldwell's chances against a man who had proven his world-class credentials on numerous occasions. The *Daily Mirror*'s Peter Wilson found it difficult to predict a winner. Pointing to the fact that Halimi had twice put in below-par performances against Belfast boxers in London – Jimmy Carson in 1957 and Gilroy seven months previously – he was still sceptical of Caldwell's ability to impress as a bantamweight. Noting that Caldwell had yet to be tested by a seasoned puncher, he felt that that moment was close at hand. In Caldwell's favour was his ability to wear down opponents through sheer boxing and ring-craft. The bottom line was, however, that Halimi, in a thirty-eight-fight career, had never lost on points.

In the *Daily Express*, Sydney Hulls suggested that Caldwell had to finish off Halimi by the ninth round, or the big-shouldered French-Algerian would come to the fore. Harking back to Halimi's crass assertion that his win over Gilroy had avenged Joan of Arc in 1431, Hulls hoped that Caldwell would be able to say that he had avenged for Ireland Halimi's victory over Gilroy. M. V. Cogley, previewing the fight in the *Irish Independent*, tried hard to pinpoint a factor which would contribute to a Caldwell victory. 'It goes against the grain to vote against "one of ours",' said Cogley, adding, however, 'it seems to me that Halimi should get on top in the closing stages, or, perhaps, force an early finish against a tiring rival.' Twenty-one was an incredibly small number of professional outings, it was noted, to have put Caldwell on the threshold of a world title.

'I've seen Halimi; I know John can beat him,' boasted Sam

Docherty to a packed press conference at Wembley Arena on Tuesday, 30 May 1961, the day of Caldwell's moment of fate. Caldwell, wearing his Irish Olympic blazer, added, 'I am convinced that Halimi is past his best and I can succeed where Freddie Gilroy failed.' It was a confident assertion by the Caldwell camp, who knew that they had nothing to lose when the bell sounded that evening. A win for Caldwell would herald the greatest night for Irish boxing since Rinty Monaghan had beaten Jackie Paterson to claim the world flyweight title in Belfast in 1949. A defeat would have been a gallant first outing in the bantamweight division.

What Caldwell had in his favour was that he had done his home-work on his opponent and would not be lacking in skill – provided he did not get drawn into a brawl with Halimi. Caldwell exuded self-assurance – not cockiness – as he went through his paces in Solomons's Windmill Street gym. The weigh-in on the morning of the fight saw Caldwell record 8st 4lb 6oz, while Halimi came in a mere four ounces under the 8st 6lb limit. Both boxers looked to be in peak condition, with the bronzed and muscular Halimi exuding supreme confidence to the press in attendance.

By early evening of the day of the fight, crowds of Irish fans were milling around Wembley Arena. Special flights from Nutts Corner airport ferried Belfast fans to London that day. Local boxing fanatic Joe McCann had provided locals with return flights to and from London for the princely sum of £10 and eighteen shillings, an amount which included tickets and overnight accommodation. It was a case of déjà vu for many of the ten thousand fans, who had travelled in vain to see Gilroy box the same man, for the same title, at the same venue, seven months earlier. However, on this occasion, there was a sneaking suspicion that a boxer of Caldwell's calibre could finish Halimi off, thereby avenging Gilroy's defeat.

In May 1961, non-smokers had not yet been invented. Wembley Arena that night was shrouded in thick smog, as thousands of cigarettes were smoked in anticipation of an Irish triumph. At the centre stood a brilliantly illuminated ring, surrounded by scores of crouching photographers with cameras primed, all waiting to capture the telling moments. The undercard was decidedly low-key. Belfast did get an early setback when Alex O'Neill lost on points to West Ham's Brian Bissmire.

Finally, at 10 PM, the moment arrived. Deafening roars accompanied the Belfast challenger, sporting his trademark crew cut, through the packed arena to the floodlit ring. Halimi, on his entrance, endured the catcalls of the Irish contingent, but looked unfazed amid the mayhem. The formal announcements were delivered as the noise rolled thunderously around the arena. The ring was cleared, and referee Ben Bril was left to deliver his final instructions to the two boxers. Caldwell and Halimi returned to their corners and, amid backslaps and final words of encouragement, gum-shields were put in place and the bell rang to signal the commencement of battle.

The two boxers touched gloves in the centre of the ring, and Caldwell went on the attack, landing two neat left hooks, which put Halimi on the back foot. Halimi countered with a right and was then cautioned for a low blow. Caldwell soon had his opponent on the ropes, and it was apparent that he was troubling the champion. By round two, Halimi had been cut. The right hand of the challenger was landing with purpose and, as the bell sounded, Caldwell had two rounds in the bag.

The third round was Halimi's, as his counterpunching came to the fore, but, in the fourth, Caldwell recovered, to shade the round. It was a tactical display of controlled boxing by Caldwell, who was refusing to enter into a punch-up. In rounds five, six and seven, Halimi went headhunting, but John's ring-craft made him an elusive target. However, Desmond Hackett of the *Daily Express* noted that Caldwell walked into a fearful punch in the sixth round that almost made the Irishman's 'eyes pop'.

By the ninth, the cut above Halimi's left eye had opened again, and Caldwell attacked with gusto, firing two-fisted flurries to keep ahead. The masses in the arena now began to believe that an upset was on the cards, with Caldwell showing all the heart and fight of a lion. Halimi's face was engorged with blood and the base instincts of the crowd came to the fore again. Desmond Hackett noted, 'As Halimi's face turned into a mask of crimson, the arena became a wild bowl of stamping and whistles – a savage accompaniment to this blood-stained fight.'

John was approaching the crucial finale of the fight in the ascendancy, but, then again, so had Gilroy – and that had ended in Irish tears. 'Box, box, box and move!' screamed Sam Docherty to Caldwell from his corner. The Belfast man was rationing his left hand, to great effect. Rounds eleven and twelve passed with Caldwell still leading. The fight entered round thirteen, the round in which Gilroy had ended up on the canvas. Halimi, a man possessed, began throwing uppercuts like a guillotine in reverse. In desperation, the champion tried to wipe his bloodied face with the thumb of his glove. Caldwell remained calm, using his skill and his fists to stay out of danger. Caldwell was living up to his nickname as, with cold eyes, he picked off his opponent without mercy. The bell rang and the crowd erupted; Caldwell was six minutes away from glory.

In the fourteenth, Caldwell again avoided a battle and, as the bell rang for the last three minutes, the crowd stood and roared in anticipation as history beckoned. Halimi needed a knockout to win. However, rather than play it safe, Caldwell went for the kill in the last round, forcing his opponent into a corner and along the ropes. Then the point of no return arrived for Halimi when a crashing left hook, followed by a right cross, sent the champion to the canvas for a count of five. The titleholder recovered, but he knew he was on the verge of losing his crown. Caldwell was almost home as he snapped out clean, precise jabs. It was now merely a matter of time for Caldwell, the delirious crowd, Belfast and Ireland. The countdown began in the arena as the moment neared. Halimi's chance was gone – seven, six, five, four, three, two, one. The bell sounded and Caldwell was surely the new world champion. For a split-second, all eyes were on the referee.

Without hesitation, the referee grabbed Caldwell's arm and raised his glove in deserved triumph. Cue pandemonium in the ring, as Docherty and a mass of Caldwell's closest friends and family stormed the ropes. Fans danced in the aisles as Wembley Arena shuddered under a riotous outburst of noise and energy. The moment had come for John Caldwell. He was the new bantamweight champion of the world.

With outstretched arms and a smile as wide as Belfast Lough, John greeted the invading masses. All those years of pain, sacrifice, self-doubt, loneliness, hurt and denial vanished for Caldwell in a singular and glorious moment. From the humble streets of the Falls Road to those splendid seconds in London, it had been a long and arduous journey. The tears of relief and ecstasy flowed. God, in his wisdom, had truly been kind to John Caldwell of Cyprus Street in Belfast at Wembley Arena on Tuesday, 30 May 1961.

Eventually, when a semblance of order returned to the ring, Caldwell received his silver globe to mark the fact that he was, to all intents and purposes, the champion of the world. The split in the NBA was merely academic, and now John held half of the disputed title. The microphone was handed to the man of the moment, who proceeded to thank Jack Solomons and Sam Docherty. The crowd cheered every sentence and, eventually, Caldwell's entourage made its way to a packed and delirious dressing room.

Halimi was gracious in defeat. 'Caldwell is a gentleman and my eye injury had nothing to do with the verdict,' said the former champion. 'He is a great boxer and I have no quarrel with the verdict.' Freddie Gilroy of Ireland – and not Joan of Arc of France – had been avenged on this occasion. In the post-mortem for the press, Caldwell gave an undertaking to give Gilroy a crack at his title 'any time he likes, providing that the price is right'. Docherty, however, was keen to give Halimi a return match, as stipulated in the contract. Amid the happiness, the hugs and the backslapping, though, there remained one glaring piece of unfinished business. That was a clash with Éder Jofre for the undisputed crown. Docherty, when asked about the prospect of a unification fight, was cautious. 'Sure, after the Halimi rematch, we'll give Éder Jofre, the American-named "world champion", a match,' he said. Caldwell agreed with his manager, pointing out that a clash with Jofre would be a certainty, 'any time, for the right money'.

The party lasted long into the night, as Ireland painted London green. Telegrams from the great and the good poured into Caldwell's hotel. In Belfast, wild scenes of celebration erupted on the Falls Road, and Caldwell's boyhood home in Cyprus Street was mobbed by well-wishers. John recalled in 2007:

> Halimi was a very, very dangerous man and a hard hitter and I know that well as he caught me many times throughout the fight. He was constantly at me – in and out all the time – and I couldn't take my eyes off him for a split second: the fight was one of the hardest of my career. I remember that after a terribly hard struggle, I eventually knocked him down in the last round and that got me the decision in the end. I felt as if I was on top of the world – which literally I was – and knew, as an Irishman, that it had been a great sporting achievement. I was the first fighter to win a world title since Rinty Monaghan, and it was everything that I could have wanted to achieve.

Two days later, John was paraded along the Falls Road. The streets were packed with well-wishers, and bunting adorned every lamp-post. People carried posters with the messages 'Welcome Home John' and 'Hail the Conquering Hero', and craned their necks to see the man show off his trophy from the back of a converted lorry. The procession was led by the St Peter's Brass Band, and the proud homecoming ended in Cyprus Street, where thousands cheered John as he returned again to his mother and father – this time as champion of the world.

Capitalising on his status was now his primary aim. A fight with Éder Jofre for the undisputed crown would be the ultimate money-spinner, but that would wait. The test Jack Solomons had set for Caldwell in order to convince himself that the Irishman was ready to fight Jofre was two fights in Wales in the space of a week, and then the rematch with Halimi. Being the golden boy of British and Irish boxing would guarantee a full house at Wembley Arena for the Halimi fight.

On 28 August, John met the French champion, Pierre Vetroff, in Carmarthen, in what was supposed to be an easy warm-up fight for the Halimi return bout. It was far from it. Vetroff was as durable an opponent as ever Caldwell had ever faced, and he took John to ten testing rounds, after which the referee awarded the Belfast champion the narrowest of points victories. Throughout the fight, Caldwell seemed perplexed by his opponent's style, and the verdict was greeted by boos from the Welsh crowd. With no world title at stake, the fight had proved to be a wake-up call for the champion, who left the ring with damage to both his eyes. 'I think the crowd was annoyed that I did not knock Vertroff out,' Caldwell said. 'They wanted too much, even from a world champion. You cannot knock them out every time.'

A week later, at the Sophia Gardens Pavilion in Cardiff, the onus was on Caldwell to produce something more akin to his outstanding form when he met Spain's Juan Cardenas. Cardenas, who in 1959 had boxed a draw with Piero Rollo for the European title, was a veteran of over ninety fights. However, he was there merely to make up the numbers. The crowd in the arena were not disappointed, as

Caldwell upped his game immensely, stopping his opponent with a vicious body shot in the eighth round. Cardenas folded like a book as he went to the canvas and had to be helped to his corner. John, who had taken control of the fight from the fourth round onwards, was upbeat afterwards, despite a bruised nose from a headbutt by his opponent. He was on course for a clash with Jofre.

For the rematch between Caldwell and Halimi, Jack Solomons was again on a financial bonanza, with a certain full house as well as a £20,000 payment from Brazilian television companies for the right to screen the bout. The fight was set for Wembley Arena on Halloween 1961. However, Solomons remained tight-lipped about his plans for a Caldwell clash with Jofre. As usual, Jolly Jack cried poverty, having spent £43 on phone calls to Jofre's manager, Abraham Katzenelson, in an attempt to secure Caldwell a clash with the Brazilian. Despite his outward loyalty to Caldwell, Solomons would have been just as content to promote a fight between Halimi and the Brazilian, should Halimi beat Caldwell in the rematch.

In Glasgow, Caldwell sparred with Billy Rafferty and Jimmy Carson and was permitted a two-day break in Belfast in early October to visit his family. On his return to Glasgow, Caldwell travelled to London and took up residence in the Thomas A. Becket gym on the Old Kent Road. Halimi arrived in London telling reporters that he had eaten only 'steaks and fortified wine' in preparation for the fight. He was supremely confident of taking back his title and curried favour with the press by visiting the Norwood Jewish Orphanage and presenting the children with a hundred complimentary tickets. In the *Irish News*, Left Lead predicted that Caldwell would 'gun down Halimi, an older man who has had his time in boxing's big time'. With the contest scheduled for fifteen rounds, Peter Wilson predicted a 'crackerjack' of a fight, though Caldwell, he added, would have his work cut out to stop his opponent.

In Belfast that Tuesday morning, legions of Irish fans boarded planes and boats, hoping to see Caldwell reinforce his claim for a crack at the undisputed title. Wembley soon creaked with over ten thousand singing fans, many well lubricated after a day out in London. However, with anticipation levels at fever pitch, the crowd was treated to a bore-fest. For the record, Caldwell won on points. The *Daily Express* labelled the bout 'shameful', while Wilson, in the *Daily Mirror*, described the fight as 'one of the worst-ever world-title battles'. He added, 'So help me, this is the first time that I have seen all three men in the ring perform with almost equal ineptitude.' The referee, Porfirio Marin of Mexico, was considered to have been as much to blame for the farce as the two boxers.

Holding, clinging, mauling and scrappy boxing were the order of the day. The crowd saw something akin to two drunken sailors trying to hold each other up. By the end of the twelfth round, it was apparent that Halimi was a spent force. What followed saw Caldwell reinforce his mediocre superiority against an opponent who – like the crowd – was happy to hear the final bell. One further moment of anguish followed for the Irish fans when the referee stalled to examine his card before eventually walking to Caldwell to raise his hand. Caldwell's win was greeted by muted cheers, but also by catcalls and the stamping of feet. The boxers blamed each other for the agony the audience had endured. Later that night, on BBC's *Sportsview*, presenter Peter Dimmock labelled both boxers 'disgraces', adding that they should have been thrown out of the ring. It had been a bad night for Caldwell, Halimi and boxing.

Regardless of the performance, it was only the result that really counted at the end of the day. And besides, the less-than-impressive showing by Caldwell may have convinced Jofre's camp that they would get an easy payday against the Irishman. In any case, Solomons had the reunification bout almost within his grasp and would not be deterred by the poor performance Caldwell had put in. In December, Caldwell voluntarily relinquished his British flyweight title; he had greater ambitions and was happy to let someone else fight for that title. Meanwhile, in São Paulo, Éder Jofre won his tenth consecutive fight when he stopped the Portuguese champion, Fernando Soto. After a series of protracted phone calls between London and São Paulo, the Caldwell-Jofre fight was eventually secured. It was announced in early December that Éder the Leader would meet Caldwell for the undisputed world bantamweight title in São Paulo on 18 January 1962.

15.

INTO THE LION'S DEN

There is an old Chinese proverb which warns us never to chase a man into his own backyard, as he may have an angry dog hidden there. For John Caldwell, the truth of that saying was about to be tested in late December 1961, when he travelled five thousand miles to Brazil for acclimatisation training in preparation for his fight with the undoubted legend that was Éder Jofre.

Born in São Paulo in March 1936, Jofre's boxing pedigree was impressive, to say the least. His Argentina-born father, Aristides, had been a lightweight boxer of note in South America who had coached the Brazilian national team at the 1948 London Olympic Games. Éder Jofre had competed for Brazil at the 1956 Melbourne Olympic Games, losing to the Chilean Claudio Barrientos in the bantamweight quarter-finals, the same division in which Freddie Gilroy had claimed a bronze medal for Ireland.

Jofre had turned professional the following year, and his hard-hitting style saw him progress eventually to glory in November 1960, when he disposed of Eloy Sanchez in six rounds to win the American version of the NBA bantamweight title. On turning professional, Jofre became a vegetarian, believing that a balanced diet of fruit, nuts and vegetables would assist him in his battle to remain at bantamweight, and provide him with stamina in the ring. He was a sporting superstar, second only in popularity to Pelé within the lexicon of Brazilian sporting heroes.

John spent Christmas of 1961 in Belfast with his family and left for Brazil from London on 27 December, accompanied by Docherty, Solomons and his stand-in trainer, Danny Holland. Holland had replaced Joe Aitcheson, with whom Caldwell did not see eye to eye. The Irishman's sluggish performance against Halimi in late October had been blamed on tension between fighter and trainer: Aitcheson's authoritarian nature had always riled Caldwell. It was reported that John had been 'sullen and silent' throughout his training in Glasgow for the Halimi fight; his heart was in Belfast. The bottom line was that John did not like Aitcheson or Glasgow, and Docherty knew that a change of trainer was required. Fortunately, Holland had been prepared to permit Caldwell to train extensively in Belfast. Solomons and Docherty knew that Caldwell had to be given a degree of freedom, since a performance similar to the one he produced against Halimi would not be good enough against Jofre.

The 30° Celsius heat in Brazil was a shock for the Caldwell camp, after the shivering cities of Belfast or Glasgow. On arrival, the Caldwell camp opted to stay in the resort of Santos, fifty miles from São Paulo. Despite the conditions, Caldwell remained upbeat, telling the assembled press in early January that, 'Everything here agrees with me, including the food.' Regarding the prospect of taking on Jofre in front of his home crowd, the Belfast champion was confident, claiming that his experience and psychological preparations would see him through. With two weeks to go until the clash, it was anticipated that four hundred British and Irish fans would undertake the gruelling trip to Brazil to cheer on Caldwell. That figure, as it turned out, was a significant overestimation, and soon the psychological tide began to turn in favour of the Brazilian.

In São Paulo, the first small victory went to Jofre's camp when Solomons conceded that the boxers would be using American-style six-ounce gloves, as opposed to the heavier European-style ones that the Belfast man had used in twice disposing of Halimi. Eventually, after much procrastination, the final contracts were signed on 8 January, with the fight to be overseen by modified NBA rules. For Caldwell, an anticipated 25 percent cut of the gate receipts and television rights was expected to net him $10,000. Also, a return match within ninety days was, according to Solomons, 'assured' within the document – at Wembley should Caldwell lose, or in São Paulo if he were to be victorious. The referee for the occasion would be former world featherweight champion Willie Pep, who had been chosen over Jack Dempsey. Three judges, one from England (Peter Wilson of the *Daily Mirror*), one from Brazil and a 'neutral' from New York were appointed to oversee proceedings. Caldwell offered to put up a side bet of £1,000 that he would beat Jofre. The Brazilian duly accepted, claiming that he would 'still be boxing at Caldwell's shadow when he hit the canvas'. It was all talk and bravado; the fight was now a guaranteed sell-out.

Nerves were fraying in Caldwell's camp. Docherty was almost incandescent when a 'best wishes' telegram arrived from the British Boxing Board. For Docherty, the telegram represented an insult to his boxer in that the Board had failed to send an official representative to look after Caldwell's interests in Brazil. 'Is this the best they can do?' demanded Docherty in front of a packed press conference. He continued:

> Caldwell is fighting for a world title and after what John has done for British boxing – and the Board – we are surely entitled to some official recognition. Win or lose, I shall be making an official protest when we get home. Rest assured, these things will not be forgotten when it comes to John being asked to fight in England again.

Despite Caldwell's outward confidence, the warning signs of what Jofre was capable of in the ring had been well documented. In Brazil, Jofre, a descendant of Portuguese, Italian and Argentinian forebears, was a superstar, and the odds-on favourite to claim the undisputed title with a partisan home crowd baying him on to victory over the Irish bantamweight. With an unbeaten record of forty-four wins, the previous eleven of which had come by way of knockout, the punching power of the so-called Golden Bantam was plain for all to see. Only twelve opponents had ever lasted the distance with Jofre, and his left hook had been nicknamed 'the sleeping drug'.

The local media was convinced that the Brazilian, with his height and reach advantage, and a noisy and parochial crowd of twenty thousand urging him on, would prove too much for Caldwell. Such was the demand for tickets to see the fight in the Ibirapuera Stadium that workers began to extend the arena in an attempt to accommodate 22,500 fight fans on the night. The gate receipts were expected to top the previous record for a sporting event in Brazil, which had been set in February 1961, when soccer side Vasco da Gama had entertained Real Madrid at the Maracanã Stadium in Rio de Janeiro. Special security measures were put in place to ensure that the arena was safe from invasion by the thousands who could not obtain a ticket. For Caldwell, the upcoming date with the man known as 'the Executioner' or 'the Gladiator' was truly a tall order. The bookmakers had made Jofre the hottest of favourites, and it would take a masterful performance by Caldwell to upset him.

Being slightly overweight, Caldwell was forced to train in heavy woollens in the blistering heat as he battled to make it under the limit. To the locals, the sight of the Belfast man going through his paces in heavy boots was quite a novelty. Everywhere he went, he was followed by photographers on motorbikes, while insults rained down on him from passersby. It was a lonely time for him. However, the arrival of his father, John, and brother, Paul, soon helped to ease his homesickness. Arriving after a three-day odyssey from Belfast to São Paulo via London, Paris, Madrid, Dakar, Montevideo and Rio de Janeiro, Paul Caldwell naturally decided it was time to go for a drink. Paul was his brother's spitting image, and he was pictured in a local hostelry with a bottle of beer in his hand. The following morning, the local papers mistakenly ran the story that John Caldwell himself had been socialising ahead of the fight. The fact that the story was erroneous did not matter a jot. The papers sold like hot cakes.

The media noted that, whilst he was superbly fit, clever and fast in the ring, Caldwell lacked the telling punch that would trouble the local hero. Each day, over a thousand locals crammed into the Wilson Russo Gymnasium to see Caldwell give a sparring master-class. In a post-training interview, one opponent, Ivan Cipriano, conceded that the Irishman 'was faster than Jofre and he jabs splendidly with his left and follows up with a right at precisely the right moment'. Despite his lesson in ring-craft, Cipriano added that Jofre, tellingly, had a far more powerful punch. Jofre's father, Aristides, was upbeat about his son's chances, maintaining that whilst Caldwell was a 'good boxer', Éder possessed the punch of Joe Louis and the skill of Sugar Ray Robinson. Asked if he was concerned about Jofre's punching power, Caldwell responded:

> No, and I don't think he worries about mine. I know he has a powerful punch, but I'd like to see him land one on me. Jofre is a great boxer, but I just consider him another opponent. There is no reason to consider him a superior boxer.

With two days to go until the fight, the Brazilian press went into overdrive when it was reported that Caldwell had received a bloody nose from his sparring partner, Raul Justo. Justo, who had been dubbed 'Flash Harry' by the British and Irish press, was a novice featherweight with just three professional fights under his belt. As a sparring partner, he had aggravated Caldwell with his arrogance and spoiling tactics. However, the news that he had drawn blood was received with glee by the Brazilian press and the Jofre camp. The fact was that the local press's reports about John's 'bloodied' nose had sensationalised what was only a very minor injury, but the irritation these reports caused him was perhaps behind the austere punishment he dished out to Justo at their next session.

Such was the ferocity of Caldwell's attacks that many of the three hundred locals present protested loudly. Docherty was overheard telling his fighter, 'Go easy on him.' The Belfast champion told the press later that he had 'persuaded Justo not to be naughty in future'. Despite Caldwell's displays of fast, powerful, skilful boxing at his final public sparring sessions, many locals suspected that the Belfast man had been pulling his punches, and it was reported that there was a 'climate of nervousness' in Jofre's camp. The psychological games were now proving crucial as the fight, and Caldwell's decisive moment, drew near.

In Ireland, a majority of pundits were convinced that Caldwell had the ability to upset the odds and defeat Jofre. Freddie Gilroy was convinced that John had the skill to take the Brazilian, provided he 'kept clear of Jofre's left hook'. Gilroy's manager, Jimmy McAree, who was acutely aware of how a Caldwell victory would benefit both him and Gilroy, with an all-Irish world-title fight, was equally confident. 'John will win this one and then Gilroy will beat him for the title,' said McAree. Fred Tiedt, silver medallist for Ireland at the Melbourne Olympic Games, noted that he had witnessed Jofre being beaten very easily at the 1956 Games and felt that the Brazilian was there for the taking. However, Belfast promoter George Connell stated that, while he hoped that John would win, he felt that the Belfast man had 'caught the tiger by the tail'. That sentiment was echoed by Irish amateur legend Terry Milligan, who felt that the Brazilian would take the fight within ten rounds because Caldwell's defence was wide open.

In order to address the heat and humidity, the fight would commence at 11 PM Brazilian time (2 AM BST). It would be broadcast live in Brazil on both television and radio. For Caldwell fans in Britain and Ireland, it would be available only on shortwave radio. With just hours to go until the fight, both boxers wound up their preparations. Jofre was cautious about being labelled the favourite, claiming he would need all his strength to see off the Irishman. For Caldwell, it had been a long, lonely and arduous month in Brazil. Bookmakers were offering 3/1 odds against an Irish victory. Looking superbly fit and seeming outwardly eager to enter the ring, John dropped his guard to the media when he declared that he would be glad when his ordeal was over, adding that he had been away from home for 'long enough'. According to trainer Danny Holland, Caldwell's best chance was to rely on his speed and stamina to get a decision on points. However, the telling factor was considered to be the Brazilian's punch, and avoiding that punch for fifteen rounds was going to be a tall order for Caldwell.

At the weigh-in, Jofre came in four ounces under the 8st 6lb limit, dispelling any speculation regarding his supposed weight problems. However, nobody in the Caldwell camp actually witnessed Jofre's weigh-in, such was the shambolic nature of the event. Caldwell had stepped onto the scales in his hotel lobby that morning and been declared four ounces under the limit. However, when the Irishman weighed in at the arena, he was recorded at twelve ounces over. Holland was dumbfounded as to how the error had been made and accused the Brazilian boxing authorities of using a defective set of scales. According to John's brother, Paul, the scales which had been installed in John's hotel had been tampered with. When they returned to the hotel later that afternoon, the scales had mysteriously vanished.

Predictably, Caldwell's weight problem caused an uproar and, for a time, there was a distinct chance that the fight would be called off.

It took an intervention by the American judge, Tony Petronella, to broker a deal which gave Caldwell thirty minutes to lose the excess weight. He was forced to do some frantic laps of the adjacent athletics track to lose the final ounces. Eventually, Caldwell weighed in under the limit, but the stress of the episode had disrupted his very precise routine. He needed to rest and regain his composure before he entered the ring, but sleep would not come in the afternoon, as adrenalin coursed through the body of the Belfast underdog.

By early evening on Thursday, 18 January, the arena at the Ginásio do Ibirapuera began to fill, and anticipation of the fight grew to fever pitch in São Paulo. As the crowds milled outside the venue, it was reported that Solomons had employed the services of 'eight strong men' from London to ensure that no mass attempt was made to break through the turnstiles. Solomons's break-even target was supposedly a gate of twenty thousand. That figure, together with the extensive television and radio fees, would make him a happy man. Caldwell's share would depend on a number of factors. In essence, he would be the last to benefit, after Solomons, Docherty and Jofre had taken their cuts. As John recounted to Jack Magowan in the *Belfast Telegraph* in 2007:

> My purse for the Jofre job was to be a percentage of the gate, plus part of the television fee, an estimated $10,000, but I never saw even half of that. Sam Docherty came into my São Paulo hotel room on the morning after the fight carrying a shoebox. There were bundles of Brazilian cruzeiro notes in the box, but I never got to count them. I never knew what I was paid for a contest.

For Caldwell, who literally wore his Irish pride on his chest, in the form of his 1956 Olympic blazer, there was another slightly annoying problem. The front cover of the official programme for the bill sported pen-pictures of Jofre and Caldwell, adorned in the Brazilian and Union flags.

As the temperature dropped to an 'acceptable' 20° Celsius, the moment arrived and Caldwell made his way to the ring amid thousands of screaming Brazilian fans. Calls of 'Kill him! Kill him!' resounded around the arena, along with whistles and jeers, as the Irishman made his way through the baying mob. He was truly a long way from Belfast. Jofre's route to the ring was a procession of adulation for a home-town hero. He sported a blue silk dressing gown with a golden cockerel on its back, and he was interviewed by Brazilian radio as he entered the ring. Jofre was outwardly indifferent to his challenger, relaxed and nonchalant about the task in hand.

The noise reached a climax as the two boxers were introduced for the fight that would finally resolve the world-bantamweight conundrum. The cards, though, were stacked massively in favour of the Brazilian as the bell rang. Caldwell, Jofre and referee Willie Pep became the centre of attention for the howling mob. Countless tens of thousands in the British Isles listened with trepidation.

The opening round was tentative, and the crowd became impatient at the lack of action. Caldwell's straight jabs were met occasionally by left shots from Jofre, but the round was mostly a limbering-up exercise for both men. In the second round, Jofre went on the attack against Caldwell's deep, crouching style and opened up with body shots, which caught John full-on. At the end of the round, John's face seemed to have been bruised. Jofre began to take command in the next two rounds, and it became plain that his punches were well above bantamweight standard. Caldwell began to clinch, and received the wrath of the Brazilian crowd for his tactics.

In the fourth, Caldwell scored with neat body blows that troubled Jofre. In round five, Jofre's punches came to the fore again and Caldwell's body took some severe punishment. Despite fighting back gamely, Caldwell was sent to the canvas for the first time in the fight and received an eight-count from the referee. The writing was now on the wall for the Irishman, but his gameness and bravery shone through; his speed and agility were still intact as the fight progressed. Jofre, however, was stalking his prey with purpose.

By the tenth round, the crowd sensed that Jofre was on the verge of victory. Buoyed by the noise, he upped his aggression levels and easily caught Caldwell with flurry after flurry of punches. With thirty seconds left in the tenth round, Caldwell had been undone, and his defence was in tatters. A vicious left hook to his face was the signal that Danny Holland needed to throw in the towel. Sam Docherty vaulted through the ropes and referee Pep stepped in to declare Caldwell a beaten man. The arena erupted; power had overcome craft. John's ordeal was over.

With hindsight, Caldwell had been well beaten. *Gazeta Esportiva* noted that 'Jofre had won by a massacre'. By the time the referee intervened, Caldwell had been overwhelmed. There had been no doubt that Jofre had been the master as he outclassed his twenty-three-year-old rival. The three judges at ringside all had Jofre well ahead at the time of the stoppage: Tony Petronella had scored the contest 89–83; Brazilian Edmar Teixeira had his fellow countryman an incredible 90–73; and England's Peter Wilson had scored the contest 88–82.

Caldwell's bravery was noted.* Referee Willie Pep described the Irishman as 'having the heart of a lion', but the manner of the defeat immediately cast doubt on the prospect of a rematch. Jofre's co-manager, George Parnassus, told the press that 'nobody would want a repetition of last night's massacre . . . Jofre's next fight will be a non-title fight in San Francisco within forty-five days against the Mexican,

---

* On being appointed Brazilian Ambassador to Ireland in 2008, Pedro Fernando Brêtas Bastos wrote to the Caldwell family expressing his admiration for John. As a young man in 1962, Bastos had been thrilled by John's performance in Brazil and had always wanted to meet the courageous little Irishman who had fought Jofre. Sadly, at that time, John was too ill to travel to Dublin. In later years, Caldwell recalled the painful reality of his clash with Jofre. 'I fought a lot of good boxers, but the man with the knowledge and the punch was Jofre . . . He was the hardest hitter of them all; when he hit you, you didn't forget it in a hurry.'

Herman Marquez'. The fact that Jofre had agreed to defend his title against Marquez in California on 20 March in a match that his camp claimed had been agreed to in 1960 and would act as a warm-up for the Caldwell rematch created a glaring problem for Caldwell. If Jofre were to lose his title to Marquez, Jofre's rematch with Caldwell would be meaningless.

Soon, Docherty and Solomons were also casting doubt on the prospect of a Caldwell-Jofre rematch. Plans which had been made for Caldwell to travel home via Argentina to secure a clash with former world champion Pascual Pérez were shelved as an immediate return to London was booked. Meanwhile, promoter Jack Solomons claimed – somewhat predictably – that the fight in São Paulo had lost him money. The 'official' attendance had been given as 16,545, which was significantly less than the anticipated twenty thousand. (The arena had been extended to accommodate 22,500, though, and Paul Caldwell recalled that 'there wasn't an empty seat in the arena and the gangways were crowded by the overspill of spectators'.) With £14,000 payable to Jofre to defend his title in England, and the comprehensive manner in which Caldwell had been defeated, it was evident that a return bout would not prove to be the money-spinner for which Solomons had hoped.

Docherty claimed that, on reflection, Caldwell had had no chance against Jofre as 'our boy had to fight Jofre and the crowd' and that any rematch would need to be on neutral ground. Sporting a bruised eye in New York, where he had stopped on the way to London, Caldwell predicted that a rematch in front of a Belfast crowd would be a different scenario. In his view, 'at least they won't jeer me – or him for that matter'. However, no date – and no undertaking – had been agreed by Jofre's camp for a return fight. Despite the 'contractual obligation' of a rematch, Solomons was vague on the timescale for the Wembley clash. In New York, Docherty stated that he and Caldwell would be staying over to discuss the prospect of a number of fights there. 'We'll fight anyone,' said Docherty, as Caldwell nodded in agreement – which seemed to further undermine the idea that a contractually guaranteed rematch with Jofre was only ninety days away.

Solomons was determined to move ahead with the rematch, though. With the contracts for Jofre's defence against Marquez exchanged, Solomons sent a cable to the Brazilian boxing association in early February, requesting that Jofre be suspended, and threatening to sue him for damages of $100,000. Faced with a legal battle that they would most likely lose, the Jofre camp reluctantly agreed to postpone the date with Marquez and defend the title at Wembley Arena on 10 April, a date that was within the original agreement for the rematch. However, problems arose when Solomons claimed that he had not been paid a promised £14,000 in television rights by the Brazilian promoters for the original fight in January, and changed the date of the rematch to 5 June to allow the money to be paid before the fight. This was the excuse the Jofre camp needed to opt out of the return bout, as the original deadline for the rematch had been breached, not by them, but by Solomons. The return match was dead, and Solomons had to make alternative plans to recoup the losses he claimed to have incurred in Brazil.

While January had been a horrible month for John Caldwell, February began on a positive note. On the first day of the month, he was inducted into the Irish sporting hall of fame at the annual Caltex Awards ceremony at Dublin's Gresham Hotel. It was a fantastic honour in recognition of his winning of the world crown against Alphonse Halimi in May of the previous year. Taoiseach Seán Lemass presented the Belfast boxer with his award on a star-studded night of celebration. Freddie Gilroy had received the same accolade in 1959. With Belfast now possessing two world-class bantamweights, who were both Olympic medallists and members of the Irish sporting hall of fame, a blind man on a galloping horse could see that it was only a matter of time before they clashed.

16.

SKULDUGGERY AND SHENANIGANS

While John Caldwell licked his wounds after the Jofre defeat, Freddie Gilroy reinforced his claim as Britain and Ireland's top bantamweight. On 3 March, Freddie scored an impressive second victory over Glasgow's Billy Rafferty at the King's Hall. It was a gruelling fight for Gilroy, which he won by knockout in round twelve, claiming the coveted Lonsdale Belt outright, since it had been the third occasion on which he had fought for and retained the title. However, the fight took more out of Gilroy than he had expected. Sporting six stitches in a cut over his left eye, he collapsed later in the evening and was rushed to hospital. After overnight observation, the twenty-five-year-old was sent home and ordered to take a full two months' rest from boxing.

Nonetheless, the victory over Rafferty was seen as a turning point for Gilroy, who had endured a crisis of confidence throughout 1961. Now Gilroy was once again in contention, and a clash with Caldwell was the no-brainer that would provide both managers, and the two boxers, with lucrative dividends. The fight was a promoter's dream. Behind the scenes, Jimmy McAree and Sam Docherty began tentative talks to secure a bout that would fill any arena in Ireland to the bursting point. Solomons knew that the matchup made sense. It would be a commercial phenomenon beyond anyone's wildest expectations, even his own.

Still holding out – at least publicly – for a rematch with Jofre, Solomons added Caldwell to his 10 April Wembley Arena bill, for a warm-up fight against Mexican Jose Lopez. All was not well, though, in the Caldwell camp, during preparations for that fight. On 20 March, all hell broke loose between Caldwell and Docherty, as the Belfast man defied an order from Docherty to train in London. John had had enough, and the Brazilian experience had left a bad taste in his mouth. He packed his bags and boarded a flight to Belfast. 'I'm fed up in London,' he said.

> At home, I'm happy and get a good square meal – in London I've had to put up with lonely accommodation above the gym and I have to eat out every night . . . I have never disputed Mr Doherty's right to be the boss and I owe him a lot, but my peace of mind is important too.

For Caldwell, Belfast offered top-class sparring and easy access to quiet country roads for running. In London and Glasgow, he had complained, his roadwork was carried out in crowded streets, in the midst of cars and buses. Most importantly, John missed his family, and that was something that Docherty refused to comprehend. At heart, John Caldwell was a homebody, and he had to be happy to be ready for the ring.

The tensions between manager and boxer had been laid bare for all to see. The *Daily Mirror*, through its opinionated boxing correspondent Peter Wilson, was particularly sensationalist in the criticism it dished out to Caldwell. Ignoring the fact that the Belfast man was melancholy and missing his wife and two young children,

Wilson ran the facetious banner headline, COLD-EYED KILLER GOES HOME TO MUM. This assertion, despite the fact that it was plainly untrue and unfair to Caldwell, was a calculated insult to the fighter's integrity.

Docherty was typically indifferent to his fighter's complaints. 'Caldwell has had far too much of his own way,' he told Wilson. 'It is up to a manager to manage his fighter and not the other way round. I have done my best for Caldwell and this is the thanks I get.' Tellingly, Docherty added: 'If Caldwell wants it this way, I have patience, but I'll wait until the agreement between us expires and then I'll tear it up.' Docherty ended his bluster by telling Wilson, 'I'll tell you one thing, Mr Wilson, if he tries to defy me, he can sit and rot. This is one case where the tail will not wag the dog.' The tough, street-wise Glaswegian within Docherty had bared his sharp teeth.

It was a massive and embarrassing public fall-out, and soon Caldwell's fight with Lopez was cancelled. The stand-off lasted a full week, with intermediaries working overtime to patch up the differences between manager and boxer. Caldwell was backed into a corner, and his options were very limited. He needed Docherty, and had to relent. On 29 March, John flew to Glasgow to apologise to Docherty for the 'inconvenience' he had caused and for making a 'nuisance' of himself. Peter Wilson, predictably, reported the apparent climb-down in all its gory detail.

It was humiliating, but not a capitulation. John was no longer going to allow Docherty to treat him like an indentured slave. The tough Glasgow bookmaker knew how much the Belfast boxer was worth to him, and there was no way he was going to let him be snapped up by anyone else. Further talks between the two men took place in Belfast three days later; Docherty relented and Caldwell was allowed to do a portion of his training in his own city. Caldwell had forced his manager to meet his demands. However, the father-son relationship between Docherty and Caldwell had been fatally damaged. For the rest of their turbulent partnership, they barely spoke.

The key to the bitterness between Caldwell and Docherty which had reared its head in March 1962 may well have been money. Caldwell never knew how much his January fight against Jofre had grossed. What he did come to learn, though, was that what he had been paid was a pittance compared with what Docherty and Solomons had pocketed. Docherty was supposed to have paid John the princely sum of £9,014 for the fight. Solomons had personally counted out that amount in cash to Docherty in Brazil. What happened, thereafter, according to Caldwell, was that Docherty gave him a shoebox full of Brazilian currency after the fight.

Caldwell should have counted the money there and then and verified the full amount, but he was young, and trusted Docherty. Theirs was an arrangement without formal contract, without receipts, based largely on a nod and a wink, and cash in hand. As John's wife Bridie recalled, 'Sam Docherty just didn't do contracts.' Caldwell accepted in good faith that his manager would pay him the majority of the earnings accrued from each fight. The Brazilian experience, though, had left him suspicious that he had been deceived – indeed, seriously cheated. That belief had irritated the boxer, as rumours abounded that Docherty and Solomons had made significant fortunes from the trip to Brazil. That, though, could never be proved; there was no paper trail. So the question remains: where did the £9,014 that Solomons gave to Docherty end up?

There is no doubt that rising to the very top of a boxing and gambling empire in a tough city such as Glasgow had required a merciless streak. Docherty's success had in no way been built on charm. A fascinating insight into the man occurred on 26 March 1962, a week after the bust-up with Caldwell. That day, John McSweeny, a messenger in Docherty's bookmaking business, lodged £9,995 to Docherty's account in the Royal Bank of Scotland in Glasgow's Jamaica Street.

The bank teller, John Prentice, a man with twelve years' experience, made a monumental blunder and gave McSweeny a receipt for £90,995. When that gaffe had been discovered, a flustered bank manager phoned Docherty, requesting that the counterfoil be returned. But Docherty did not return it. He commenced legal proceedings against the bank for £81,000, claiming that the bank teller had stolen that amount.

The case came to court in Glasgow a year later. Docherty claimed that he had given £90,995 in cash to McSweeny to lodge, a sum the bookmaker claimed he had accumulated from boxing shows in Ireland and by betting on Caldwell to become world champion. In addition, he produced a witness, a Dublin accountant named Vincent MacEoin, to testify that he had provided Docherty with a £50,000 loan in cash, a sum which formed part of the amount that McSweeny was supposed to have lodged. All these claims were corroborated in court by Docherty's accountant, Gerald Woodlard. Judgement was reserved for two months.

On 17 May 1963, Lord Cameron gave his verdict on the case. It did not make good reading for Docherty. The bookmaker had, according to Cameron, 'deliberately advanced what he knew to be a false and fraudulent claim and advanced it with perjured evidence'. In addition, the judge said that he was 'not prepared to accept his [Docherty's] haziness of memory' throughout the case. Regarding Docherty's story on how he had obtained his fortune, the judge pointed out that the bookmaker 'had been less than frank' in his relationship with the Inland Revenue. Docherty's accountant, Gerald Woodlard, was, added Cameron, 'only a less satisfactory witness than his employer' and had been 'intentionally misleading'.

Most damningly, Cameron indicated that, in deciding whether to believe Prentice, the bank clerk, or McSweeny, Docherty's messenger, he had taken into account the fact that McSweeny had a criminal record stretching back to 1922. Indeed, in 1944, McSweeny had incurred the dubious and rare distinction of being declared an official 'outlaw', for refusing to appear in court to answer a charge of safe breaking. The judge found that Docherty had been ruthless in trying to capitalise on a clerical error, and threw out Docherty's claim. No appeal was lodged.

In 1967, Caldwell sued Docherty for £15,000, a sum he claimed he was owed for his boxing. Without a receipt or contract, Caldwell, not surprisingly, lost this case. The opening day in court was reported in the *Glasgow Herald* on 21 May 1967. Docherty defended his integrity, claiming he had treated Caldwell fairly throughout his career. In an adjacent article that day, it was reported that a Glasgow man with fourteen previous criminal convictions had been sent to the High Court on charges of possessing £35,000 in forged savings stamps. That man, who was employed as a bookmaker's clerk, was the same John McSweeny who had claimed to have acted in good faith and lodged £90,995 on Docherty's behalf in March 1962. Caldwell never really stood a chance against Docherty and his ilk.

17.

RUNNING OUT OF OPTIONS

With a tenuous peace now re-established between Caldwell and Docherty, Solomons reinstated the Belfast boxer to the 10 April Wembley bill. Caldwell returned to the ring against the Italian journeyman Federico Scarponi, an inexperienced replacement for Lopez. Promoted under the title 'Champions on Parade', that bill was headlined by Caldwell, welterweight Brian Curvis and a clash between Howard Winstone and Derry Treanor for the British featherweight crown. It was, for Caldwell, a mundane dose of boxing reality after the hype of the clash with Jofre.

John was far from impressive in his laboured ten-round victory. He lacked authority and seemed reluctant to lash out at his opponent when he seemed to have him at his mercy. While the Italian did not unduly worry Caldwell, he was the type of opponent who really should not have been considered worthy to step inside the ropes with the Irishman. What purpose the outing achieved for Caldwell, besides exposing his ring-rustiness, is hard to fathom. There was no doubt that, on that April night, he was not even a shadow of the boxer who had gone toe to toe with Jofre in January.

Within a week of Caldwell's victory over Scarponi, a deal to arrange the inevitable clash of Ireland's top bantamweights was in the process of being sealed. 'It was a promoter's dream,' recalled Jack Magowan of the *Belfast Telegraph*, adding that it was to be the 'most combative match in Ireland since Brian Boru squared up to the invading Danes'. On 17 April, Solomons flew to Belfast to negotiate the purse for the fight. He became locked in four hours of talks, as the boxers' managers held out for the best deal possible.

The chief bargaining chip Solomons carried was a 'guaranteed' match for the winner against Éder Jofre. Since Freddie Gilroy's British and Empire titles would be at stake, Jimmy McAree was determined to extract the lion's share of the purse. Solomons left Belfast without a deal, telling the press he could 'nearly buy the King's Hall for what Jimmy McAree wanted'. Negotiations continued over the next ten days until, finally, on 30 April, it was reported that a deal had been struck, with the fight scheduled to take place in either Dublin or Belfast on 29 June.

Solomons, who would co-promote the contest with George Connell, announced that he would be travelling to Ireland to view venues in order to choose the one that could accommodate the biggest crowd. The arena tipped to host the fight was Dalymount Park on the north side of Dublin. The home of Bohemians soccer club, it could hold at least forty thousand spectators. It was obvious that money would be the principal driving force behind the fight. In *The Ring* that month, Caldwell had been ranked as number two in the world bantamweight ratings; Gilroy was at number five. Solomons described the contest as 'the best even-money fight ever'.

The contest would provide the biggest payday for Solomons since he had promoted the Eric Boon vs. Arthur Danahar British lightweight title fight at the Harringay Arena in 1939. That bout was the first fight ever to be televised live by the BBC, and it made history as it was screened in cinemas across London. A sure sign of the hype the Caldwell vs. Gilroy clash would generate was provided when

Solomons stated that he would pay the expenses of former world heavyweight champion Jack Dempsey to travel from the United States to referee the contest. Solomons even offered to pay the expenses of the British referee who would be deprived of a night's work should Dempsey get the nod from both camps.

On 4 May, Jofre had defended his world title successfully against Marquez, stopping him two minutes and fifteen seconds into the tenth round. Caldwell's challenge had lasted thirty seconds longer in January, but a rematch with Jofre was now a distant and diminishing hope. Within days, contracts for the Caldwell-Gilroy fight were exchanged. Solomons and Connell were to be joint promoters at the King's Hall in Belfast.* Connell had squeezed seventeen thousand spectators into that venue in 1959 when Gilroy had beaten Peter Keenan for the British title, and similar attendance was expected for this contest.

At a 7 May press conference in Belfast's Grand Central Hotel, Solomons and both camps were predictably buoyant about the fight. Solomons, upbeat after his beloved Tottenham Hotspur had beaten Burnley in the FA Cup final that weekend, assured the press that either Éder Jofre or Alphonse Halimi would box the winner in

* While the fight was eventually set for the King's Hall, Solomons had scouted sites in Dublin, too. He arrived in Dublin on 1 May and was met by his agent, Mike Callahan, and the Belfast promoter George Connell. They viewed Tolka Park in Drumcondra and then travelled the short distance to Dalymount. While Solomons was impressed with these, he was won over by the potential of the facilities he saw at Lansdowne Road, headquarters of the Irish Rugby Football Union. Having promoted massive outdoor events at the White City Stadium in London, he felt the rugby stadium was perfect for the clash. He anticipated that a crowd of fifty or sixty thousand could be accommodated in the stands and on the pitch, for what would be the biggest fight ever staged in Ireland. In Belfast, the Oval, home of Irish League side Glentoran, was also under consideration, but this was an occasion that demanded the biggest possible venue, and Lansdowne Road ticked all the boxes. In the end, though, with the overheads involved in transforming a football ground into a boxing arena, and the risk of an open-air venue being a washout, Belfast's King's Hall was chosen as the venue.

Belfast. To Solomons and Connell, holding the Caldwell-Gilroy fight in Belfast was an 'absolute natural'. It was announced that ringside seats would cost six guineas – approximately £120 in 2014 prices. Solomons wisecracked that he had spent so much time in Ireland that he was changing his name to 'O'Solomons'. He said the fight would be the most expensive ever staged in Ireland, and suggested that the King's Hall had been chosen at the request of the two boxers, adding, 'When two fighters fight for me, they become my partners in a business enterprise and have an equal say where they should fight.' Gilroy, as titleholder, had been promised 27 percent of the gate, while Caldwell would receive 23 percent.

The two boxers then addressed the assembled media. Caldwell spoke briefly, saying, 'I was once a British flyweight title and world-title holder: now I feel lonely without those belts. I am glad that this fight is for Freddie's titles.' When Gilroy spoke, it was evident that, underneath the perceived camaraderie of two local boxers, there would be an element of animosity in the ring. 'John and I are pretty good friends, and we will be right up for the fight,' Gilroy said. Pointedly, he added, 'Then inside the ring we will hate each other, but I hope we can be good friends afterwards.' For Gilroy, Caldwell was the man who had stepped in and taken what he felt had been his – namely the right to a rematch with Halimi. This was a grudge match, and all notions of friendship would be eclipsed, as serious money further poisoned their relationship.

Two weeks after the press conference announcing the fight, Caldwell and his wife, Bridie, were almost killed when their car skidded off the main Belfast-to-Dublin road, just outside the town of Swords. After being treated for shock, they were released from hospital, but it had been a close escape. The incident, however, did not stop Caldwell from appearing in an exhibition bout in Cork the following evening against the Irish lightweight John Martin. Sporting a slight elbow injury, Caldwell received a rousing reception in the

Gurranabraher Parochial Hall as he displayed his full array of skills and trickery.

The deal struck for the Caldwell-Gilroy fight had obliged Gilroy to appear in a Solomons-promoted warm-up bout against Frenchman René Libeer on 5 June at Wembley. It was an arrangement that would have a direct impact on Gilroy's date with Caldwell just over three weeks later. Libeer, who held the French bantamweight crown, had sent Caldwell to the canvas twice in their clash at Wembley two years earlier. Caldwell had outpointed Libeer on that occasion, but it was evident that the Frenchman could pose a threat to Gilroy. For Solomons, the fight with Libeer would be a perfect opportunity for fight fans to compare how Gilroy and Caldwell had measured up against the Frenchman. Jimmy McAree pointed out to the press that 'a warm-up contest against a pushover is a waste of time'. Gilroy, who had lost almost two stone in preparation for the fight, told the media he was 'swinging' in anticipation. Solomons, though, publicly exercised caution by claiming that he had asked Freddie not to box at all, and that it was the Belfast fighter who had insisted on taking the fight on.

The clash with Libeer was a needless one, and it left unanswered many questions about Gilroy's ability to prepare effectively for the clash with Caldwell. The first problem occurred when Gilroy weighed in at 8st 10lbs, four pounds over the bantamweight limit. He was forced to pay a forfeit of £50 to Solomons. Although he had a weight advantage of half a stone in the ring, Gilroy was sluggish throughout the contest. The Frenchman, who, like Caldwell, had claimed a bronze medal in the flyweight class at the 1956 Olympics, won the first two rounds with ease, and it was apparent that Gilroy was, at best, only half-fit.

It was a scrappy fight, with both boxers deploying holding and mauling tactics, which drew a chorus of slow handclapping from a less-than-impressed audience. Once the Frenchman's initial onslaught had been contained, though, Gilroy began to out-box his opponent. The result was never in doubt after the fourth round. When the decision went in Gilroy's favour, McAree called it a satisfactory night and said the exercise had been just what his boxer needed prior to his clash with Caldwell. However, it was an indifferent and dour performance by Gilroy, which left many pundits bewildered.

Gilroy's problem ahead of the Caldwell clash was getting down to the agreed 8st 6lb weight. He had, perhaps, outgrown the bantamweight division. Between fights, he had ballooned to twelve stone, and had to endure weeks of physical and mental torture to make the weight. It bordered on the dangerous. Six weeks of salad and pain were part and parcel of his pre-fight build-ups, but sometimes his body refused to shed the excess weight. Gilroy's inability to make the weight for the Libeer clash worried Solomons. For a champion like Gilroy, to come in well over the weight was seen as very unprofessional. Solomons contacted the Gilroy camp and requested that a £1,000 forfeit be put in place to offset any loss he might incur should the fight with Caldwell be postponed due to weight problems. McAree's response to Solomons, as quoted in the *Belfast Telegraph*, was sharp and to the point: 'Tell Jack to go and jump in the lake!'

On 10 June, conspiracy theorists had a field day when the Gilroy camp announced that their man had injured his right hand during his bout with Libeer. Solomons was angry, claiming that he had asked Gilroy not to box Libeer at all, but that the Belfast man had insisted. Gilroy's fight with Caldwell was off. It was McAree who broke the news: 'He went to punch a heavy bag in the gym on Friday night and the pain was so bad that we took him to a doctor.' Sporting a plastered right hand, Gilroy was out of the fight, but, conveniently, not because of an inability to make the weight. Three days later, Dr Paddy McHugh of the British Boxing Board examined Gilroy's hand and found that he had displaced three small bones and had stretched ligaments. The prognosis was not good. The doctor ordered Gilroy not to train for three months. Solomons reluctantly – and suspiciously, no doubt – cancelled the King's Hall bill and rescheduled it for Saturday, 20 October.

The fight was, however, still in jeopardy as the summer progressed and Gilroy's hand injury was slow to heal. Soon, a war of words erupted between the two boxers in the local papers. Caldwell went on the offensive, claiming he was 'fed up' with waiting for Gilroy's hand to heal, and suggesting that Gilroy was running scared. 'Nonsense,' responded Gilroy. 'I want to be punching my hardest for this fight . . . Why should I duck Caldwell? I am the champion and I am getting well paid to fight him.' In August, with three months to go before the bout, Gilroy weighed well over eleven stone. For McAree, the key to getting down to the weight lay in roadwork, which Gilroy began in early September. 'The weight will tumble off him,' said McAree.

As summer turned to autumn, both boxers had begun their preparations in earnest. By 6.30 each morning, Gilroy was pounding the country roads on the outskirts of Belfast, trying to shed the four stone he had piled on. Caldwell was starting his days by attending Mass in Glasgow. The fight, as expected, was a sell-out. With a week to go, Gilroy weighed 9st 7lb, and it was decided that he would go to Dublin to lose the extra stone in a sauna. As media interest increased, it was noted that Gilroy had never looked as fit. On Wednesday, 17 October, Caldwell arrived in Belfast with his Glasgow entourage. His trainer, Joe Aitcheson, who had been relegated to bucket man at the expense of Danny Holland, commented that Caldwell was 'fitter and faster than ever – and getting better every day'. Gilroy was more forthright, telling the assembled hacks in the St John Bosco gym, 'Don't expect it to go fifteen rounds.' The waiting was almost over.

18.

THERE ARE NO LONGER WINNERS, ONLY SURVIVORS

Belfast, on the morning of Saturday, 20 October 1962, awoke to a fine autumn day. Within a week, four men from Liverpool, known collectively as The Beatles, would enter the British pop charts for the first time with their single 'Love Me Do'. The world would henceforth change, and change utterly. In Rome, the Second Vatican Council was getting under way, and the *Irish News*, to the relief of its loyal Catholic readership, was reporting that Italian detectives were 'carefully monitoring' the movements of the Reverend Ian Paisley in St Peter's Square, 'in case he tried to disrupt proceedings'. Meanwhile, Armageddon was at hand. That very week, the world was on the verge of nuclear war, as the USA and the USSR stood at loggerheads in the Cuban Missile Crisis.

Nevertheless, life continued as normal in Belfast, as final preparations were made at the King's Hall for the clash of the two local superpowers. From early morning, the south Belfast arena was alive with familiar sounds as the final preparations were made and the start time drew ever closer. The noises of hammers and drills were interspersed with the testing of public-address systems, while a plethora of officials of varying importance, with obligatory clip-boards, ran through mandatory checks. On the previous evening, a full-scale rehearsal had taken place in the hall, with hundreds of stewards, car-parking attendants and programme sellers put through their paces.

For the first time ever, the extensive car-parking facilities at the rear of the King's Hall would be opened for a boxing bill, as almost a thousand cars were expected. It was a sure sign that the middle classes had been captivated by the prospect of the clash. Throughout the day, business would be brisk in the bookmaking shops of Belfast. The odds, though fluctuating, leaned slightly towards a Caldwell victory. The Falls Road man had also been tipped for victory that morning by Jack Magowan in the *Belfast Telegraph*, which, in the spirit of the day, had published a 'sporting special' for its readership. In the *Irish News*, however, Left Lead favoured Gilroy, 'the harder puncher', to take the honours. The fight remained too close to call.

A mile from the King's Hall, at Windsor Park, police were putting in place arrangements in anticipation of the arrival of fifty-eight thousand spectators for the soccer clash between Northern Ireland and England in the British Championship. Parking restrictions were imposed within a five-mile radius, and spectators were warned not to leave their transistor radios visible in their cars, as thieves were expected to be out in force. By lunchtime, the thoroughfares around the ground were thronged with spectators eager to see if their local heroes could beat England at the Belfast venue for the first time since 1927. It was, alas, not to be for Northern Ireland, led by Danny Blanchflower, as England failed to read the proverbial script and triumphed by three goals to one.

As the football match concluded, crowds were already forming at the King's Hall, where the race for the best seats in the balcony became the number-one concern. At 6.30 PM, the doors opened and the hall began to stir with spectators, creating the beginnings of a crescendo of noise that was due to peak three hours later. Caldwell and Gilroy would not arrive at the arena until at least 9 PM; they would finish their final psychological and physical preparations in the privacy of their own local gyms. In the King's Hall, a procession of supporting contests began, but the crowd was strangely subdued: it seemed that everyone was saving their emotions for the fight.

In his programme notes, co-promoter George Connell wrote that, 'Frankly, it would be easier to guess the number of sweets in a jar than to estimate how many fans will watch tonight's "classic".' Predicting that that number could top fifteen thousand, Connell wondered where an arena could be found which would accommodate the winner's clash with Éder Jofre. In Jack McGowan's programme notes, he pointed out that, since the bust-up between Caldwell and Docherty, the two had scarcely passed the time of day. These were 'hardly satisfactory circumstances for any fighter to prepare for a title fight in', McGowan wrote. Bill Rutherford of *The People* suggested that all talk of the clash being a 'hate fight' could be banished. It was merely a clash which had to take place between Gilroy and the apprentice plumber who had succeeded him as Irish flyweight champion in 1956. Most notably – and perhaps ironically – within the programme was an advertisement for the Belfast Artificial Teeth Hospital, where a double fracture could be fixed for as little as eight shillings.

First into the ring were Belfast veterans Sammy Cowan and Paddy Graham, in a clash that Cowan won, as Graham, who was in the twilight of his career, retired in his corner at the end of the second round. This contest was followed by two fights which saw international boxers take the honours over Belfast opponents. In the first, Boswell St Louis, the talented journeyman from Trinidad, outpointed Jim 'Spike'

McCormack, while Ghana's Dennis Adjei proved too fast and accurate for Peter Lavery. With less than an hour to go until the main event, Alex O' Neill provided some comfort for the Falls Road contingent with a neat victory over Danny Lee of Glasgow. The final bout of the undercard saw Eddie Shaw, who would find fame as Barry McGuigan's trainer, display his class as he easily disposed of Sheffield's Neil Hawcroft.

By this time, the arena was full and the chanting had begun. Through a pungent fog generated by Gallaher's Blues, Park Drive and Player's Navy Cut cigarettes, countless thousands of eyes peered towards the back of the arena, trying to catch a glimpse of either Freddie Gilroy or John Caldwell. Eventually, the lights dimmed and, after a prolonged moment, a roar embraced the arena as Caldwell, the challenger, was caught in the spotlight. All around the King's Hall, balancing precariously on top of their wooden seats, men strained to see their hero. From the balcony, a wall of sound rolled over the hall, as the occasion began to match the pre-fight hype.

Along the narrow aisle, Caldwell's entourage made slow but steady progress through the illuminated scrum, as thousands of cheers and whistles threatened to test the foundations of the building. For his supporters, Caldwell was a hero, representing the Falls Road, coming home to prove a point – and his greatness. This was their chance to show their appreciation for the man who had taken a world title and fought so bravely against Éder Jofre earlier in the year. However, the majority in the hall were not Caldwell supporters. From them, a chorus of boos and catcalls rang out as the Glasgow-based fighter made his way towards the ring. For the neutral, Gilroy was the true Belfast boy, while Caldwell had chosen to leave his native city. Caldwell had a lot of hearts to win over.

The crescendo of noise came to a climax as Caldwell reached the ring and, after a momentary lull, the roar came back with a vengeance as he climbed through the ropes. He danced confidently towards the centre of the ring to acknowledge his adoring fans. He smiled as he went through his paces – the epitome of cheerful confidence. This was his moment, his big chance of redemption as he stood momentarily under the heat of the dazzling spotlights with his arm raised in acknowledgement. However, there was work to be done and, after such a reception, it was time for composure and contemplation. The roars dissolved slowly into a raucous chant of 'Johnny! Johnny! Johnny!' as Caldwell threw a combination of shadow punches and made for his corner. The advice given to him by his seconds would be lost somewhat in the din as the challenger sat waiting for Freddie Gilroy to arrive.

Within moments, the champion's entry was greeted with a decidedly superior reception, as the spotlight fell on the Gilroy camp in the corner of the arena. Gilroy's fans were most definitely in the majority. Again, a colossal noise engulfed the arena. The spotlight captured the Ardoyne man's methodical progress. Gilroy was effectively on home territory. He had built up a significant following through his nine appearances at the south Belfast venue and was definitely the favourite of the neutrals in the hall. He was, after all, the British and Empire champion. Eventually, referee Andy Smyth called the two protagonists to the centre of the ring to remind them of how he wished them to interpret the Queensberry Rules. The fighters touched gloves and went back to their corners as the crowd erupted again.

The moment had arrived. Gilroy glanced briefly towards the heavens. Caldwell blessed himself. The bell sounded. Would Gilroy be able to display the stamina he needed after the weight loss he had endured? Would Caldwell's craft see him home? A scrap would suit Gilroy: he knew that the fight had to be won before the tenth. For the purists following the challenger, a clean boxing match would suit Caldwell. The two boxers went at each other with gusto in the opening minute. It soon became clear that strategy was largely irrelevant:

it was hit and hit all the way. The noise ebbed and flowed as each man tried to establish dominance. The exchanges were fierce, with no quarter given. It was three minutes of total boxing.

Gilroy showed none of the lethargy he had displayed against Libeer; Caldwell was described as a 'restless gypsy', trying desperately to expose Gilroy to his searching right hand and combinations. The champion, however, stood his ground, catching Caldwell with a sweet left hook to the jaw that momentarily unbalanced the challenger, sending him to the canvas briefly. When Caldwell lost his composure, the crowd rose as one, but he was made of sterner stuff and was soon back in his stride. He recovered so quickly, and tore into Gilroy with such ferocity, that it was difficult to believe that the blip had even occurred. The bell sounded and the boxers returned, through the noise, to their corners. Gilroy had shaded the round, which had exceeded all expectations. The *Belfast Telegraph*'s Jack Magowan described the opening three minutes as 'the best ever', and wrote that they had reduced the crowd to 'a state of gibbering, uncontrolled hysteria'.

The fight became even more frantic, as courage and determination were displayed in abundance. As boxing writer Roger Anderson noted, 'This was a clash of ring titans; a furious blood-stained epic so frighteningly intense that the King's Hall was in danger of self-combustion.' The two bitter former friends fought like alley cats, cheered on by a frenzied crowd trapped in an occasion where mercy had vanished. In the second and third rounds, Gilroy's body punches began to dictate matters. With only seconds left in the third round, however, Caldwell exploded a right hand onto Gilroy's chin, and the champion was in trouble. The bell intervened to allow Gilroy to recover.

In the sixth, however, Caldwell again connected with a vicious right to the jaw, but, by that stage, Caldwell's strength had been sapped and Gilroy walked off the effects of the blow. It was Gilroy who was dictating the fight, throwing fierce and sustained two-handed salvos which landed with increasing accuracy on Caldwell's frail body. Time and time again, he landed crippling blows cleanly on Caldwell's ribs; the challenger did not flinch, but the crowd could sense that he had been hurt. Gilroy was the clear leader, but then Caldwell began to get a second wind and out-boxed the champion to even up the contest.

By the end of the seventh round, the fight was too close to call, with the tantalising prospect remaining of a further eight rounds of all-out action in store. The real drama of the fight, however, was merely moments away. Again, the two boxers began by thrashing away at each other in the middle of the ring. The fight had surpassed the description 'classic'. It was now a battle to the bitter end. And then, from within the ring came the unmistakable, sickening, hollow sound of bone against bone. There had been a clash of heads as the boxers broke from their clinch, and Caldwell had come off worse. Much worse. From over his right eye, a trickle of blood was noted by all in the arena; it soon became a torrent. The tide had turned in favour of Gilroy. Each punch to Caldwell's cut would reduce the ability of the challenger to continue. As the bell sounded at the end of the round, Caldwell returned to his corner in a state of panic.

Caldwell's cut man was supposed to be the best in the business. Danny Holland had been brought over from London to deal with just such an eventuality, and he battled frantically to stop the flow of blood as the official doctor looked on anxiously. Around the arena, there was collective pessimism about Caldwell's ability to continue. In the sixty seconds allocated him, Holland applied copious amounts of adrenalin and Vaseline to Caldwell's eye to address what he, and most likely Caldwell, knew was a hopeless cause. Bravely, Caldwell, who needed stitches, not Vaseline, stood to face Gilroy in what was to be a do-or-die ninth round.

The bell sounded. Gilroy could sense victory; for Caldwell, the goal was damage-limitation. Gamely, the Falls Road man threw punch after punch to keep Gilroy at bay, but the champion had time on his side and waited for his chance to connect with Caldwell's bleeding eye. Afterwards, Caldwell would say of the ninth round, 'I was just hitting him from memory, as I could neither see nor breathe; my castle just crumbled beneath me.' The cut had been breached again and was pumping blood onto Caldwell's face, body and shorts – and the white canvas of the ring. It was hopeless. The bell sounded for what would be the last time.

Caldwell went back to his corner. Holland's efforts had been in vain. As the doctor arrived at ringside, Caldwell's corner knew that the game was up. Blood was running from Caldwell's right eye and nose into his mouth; his eyesight was all but gone. With a wave of his hand, the referee signalled that Caldwell could not continue. The Ardoyne contingent began a mass celebration; most of Caldwell's Falls Roads supporters stared for a moment in disbelief and then headed off into the chilly autumn night.

The ring was pandemonium as family members and supporters tried to get to their heroes. First over to Caldwell was Gilroy, who threw his arms around his friend in sympathy. It had been an unsatisfactory end to a classic fight. The two men posed for the cameras, but it was a false show of camaraderie. The fight, as well as opening up a serious cut over Caldwell's eye, had opened up a bitter gulf between the men. A rematch was the obvious way to resolve the rivalry, and promoter Jack Solomons, at ringside, puffed contentedly on his cigar as he contemplated the prospect.

Under the spotlights, a bruised and bloodied John Caldwell was distraught, but Gilroy had retained his titles, and he was not complaining about the manner of the victory. Eventually the ring was cleared. Caldwell exited it with his mutilated head wrapped in a gory towel. The two contingents made their ways to their dressing rooms at the back of the arena. Gilroy's room was packed full of well-wishers giving hugs and backslaps; all stood and applauded him for a full minute.

The atmosphere in Caldwell's well-guarded dressing room was muted. The sounds of celebration and victory cheers pierced painfully through the door. Muhammad Ali once said, 'No one knows what to say in the loser's locker room.' That was certainly true that night in Caldwell's. As he sat silently amid the loneliness of defeat, accepting the further pain of stitches from a doctor – and some hollow comfort from a priest – the bitter taste of tears mingled with congealing blood to add to the finality of his defeat.

For Gilroy, it had been a good night. For Connell and Solomons, it had been an excellent night. For Caldwell, it had been a sad night. Eventually, he left the King's Hall with his family and walked into a Belfast night as black as his despair.

19.

'THIS WAS NOT BELFAST, THIS WAS A JUNGLE CLEARING'

On Monday, the sports pages were positively purring as they tried to put into words the essence of what had been a murderous and unforgettable battle. MEMORABLE CIVIL WAR IN BELFAST was how the *Irish Independent*'s M. V. Cogley described it. The fight, he noted, 'had caused more tension and feeling in that ring than many another title fights between Irish champions and "foreign" invaders'. For Desmond Hackett of the *Daily Express*, the brutal contest, which, he suggested, could have left the spectators with 'cauliflower eyes', had been nine rounds of 'black hate' and 'blood lust'. Wrote Hackett:

> This was not Belfast, this was a jungle clearing where two young warriors had stripped for a fight to the death . . . It was a thing of horror which brought you to the edge of your feet, hypnotised your attention on this torture pitch of two victims and two executioners.

Frank McGhee's piece in the *Daily Mirror* appeared under the banner headline GILROY SURVIVES ON NIGHT OF RAW HATE, an assertion which laid bare the proceedings over nine rounds. It had truly been an epic encounter, and had already entered into the annals as the greatest fight ever witnessed in a Belfast ring. McGhee wrote, 'I have never known a fight quite like it for pace and punch from explosive start to controversial finish.' He added that, at the time of the stoppage, the 'visibly wilting' Gilroy would have had to put in the 'performance of his life' to have lasted the full distance. Jack Magowan of the *Belfast Telegraph* summed up the encounter in his own inimitable and poetic style:

> Friends for years, now glowering foes, the pair fought like alley cats, like cocks in a pit, no mercy shown, no time for deep-laid strategies or fooling around. It was hit or be hit, and to his credit, referee Andy Smyth let them get on with it.

Gilroy thought Caldwell's tactics had been wrong from the very start of the fight. Caldwell had opted to engage Gilroy in a brawl, which left Gilroy, as the heavier puncher, with a distinct advantage. 'I knew exactly how I was going to box him that night, and I was surprised when he chose to mix it with me,' recalled Gilroy in 2005.

> I had expected him to box clever and to use every square foot of the ring. Instead, he chose to go headhunting and to try and roughhouse it with me, and that was a mistake . . . I dropped John with a left hook in round one, a good punch which seemed to embarrass more than hurt him. It clearly upset his game plan.

With hindsight, the fight had been a complete waste of time for Freddie. Ultimately it had destroyed their friendship and proved nothing.

> I didn't want to fight John Caldwell, for I felt at the time that it was a stupid fight to take. The media had built up the fight, as they had

nothing else to do, I recall that the King's Hall was heaving that night and, to be truthful, I would have loved to have been in the crowd to have savoured the moment.

In 2006, Caldwell acknowledged that he had been drawn into a battle with a heavier puncher, which was clearly costly. The bottom line, though, was that the result was inconclusive, and the chattering masses, to this day, debate what would have happened if the fight had lasted the distance. Would Gilroy, who had 'boiled down' to make the weight, have had the strength to sustain six more savage rounds? We will never know.

> I truly thought I was ahead when the fight was stopped . . . The fight was very nasty and my plans had been upset by the severity of the battle, our heads were constantly clashing, but I felt that I was getting stronger and would have taken the decision had the fight continued.

In later years, Caldwell was reluctant to talk about the intricacies of the battle with Gilroy. Asked how many people were in the King's Hall that night, he smiled and responded, 'I'm not sure, I didn't get to count all the spectators; Freddie kept me too busy.'

By the time the last satisfied punter had left the King's Hall that Saturday night, talk of a rematch was on everyone's lips. Sam Docherty told the press that a return fight was 'a must', adding that Caldwell would fight 'anytime, anywhere, and for any side stake Gilroy wishes to name.' Tellingly, Jack Solomons began to renege on the prospect of the winner being matched with Éder Jofre, saying he 'would like to see a rematch before such a clash was finalised'. A further episode of the Caldwell-Gilroy saga would, Solomons said, 'prove conclusively who the right man was to fight for the world title'. Jolly Jack added:

Gilroy is a great champion and will prove to be a great world champion. I don't remember seeing a better fight, and Caldwell must get another chance . . . The return would be the crowd-puller of all time, and I intend to put it on.

The problem for Solomons was that, although he maintained that Jofre owed him a rematch with Caldwell, the Brazilian had bigger fish to fry. Any claim Solomons had on the Brazilian was effectively null and void.

Since January 1962, Jofre had twice successfully defended his undisputed bantamweight crown. He was pure box office and was rated, pound for pound, as the best boxer on the planet. His horizons were ever-expanding; he had just signed a very lucrative contract to defend his crown in Tokyo in April 1963, against Katsutoshi Aoki. To get Jofre to London to defend his title, Solomons would have to pay the Brazilian at least £14,000 – plus four first-class return fares from Rio de Janeiro for his entourage. Solomons was acutely aware that matching either Gilroy or Caldwell against Jofre would not provide the crowd-puller he needed to cover his costs. Jofre was untouchable and improving with each performance; Caldwell and Gilroy were not in his class any more. As such, Solomons was reluctant to take a risk on the fight.

It seemed that a rematch between the Belfast battlers was the safest bet for a shrewd promoter and, importantly, bookmaker. There was, however, another good option. While the world bantamweight crown was in the secure ownership of Éder Jofre, the European belt had been claimed by the thirty-five-year-old Sardinian Piero Rollo. Rollo, whom Gilroy had beaten to become European champion in 1959, had been stopped by Éder Jofre in March 1961 after nine rounds in Brazil, in a clash for the then vacant NBA bantamweight crown. In October 1962, Rollo had reclaimed the European title from Alphonse Halimi, but he was really a veteran in the twilight of his career. Matching Rollo with Gilroy in early 1963 presented a further winnable proposition for Solomons. Both boxers could only wait while Jolly Jack weighed up his options.

By December 1962, matters got more complicated between the Caldwell and Gilroy camps. That month, the bible of boxing, *The Ring* magazine, ranked Caldwell above Gilroy in the world bantamweight rankings, despite the outcome of the King's Hall battle. As such, Caldwell had, theoretically, a better claim to be matched against either Jofre or Rollo. Meanwhile, Jimmy McAree dismissed all talk of a Gilroy-Caldwell rematch, saying, 'Caldwell has had his chance; we'd rather fight Rollo for the European title than risk two titles against Caldwell.'

Good news soon arrived for Gilroy: the European Boxing Board nominated him as the number-one contender for Rollo's European title and ordered that the fight take place by June 1963. Before that contest could be contemplated, however, the British Boxing Board intervened and ordered Gilroy to defend his British title against Caldwell no later than the middle of April. That fight went to purse, and the contract was awarded to Jack Solomons, who planned to promote the bill again in conjunction with George Connell at the King's Hall. The London bookmaker now had both Caldwell and Gilroy under contract to him; both boxers' career options were somewhat limited, with Mr Boxing now holding them to account.

John Caldwell's return to the ring took place at the Royal Albert Hall on 12 February. He was to fight Frenchman Michel Atlan on a Solomons-promoted bill as the British Isles shivered through the worst winter in almost a century. Atlan, who, at twenty-nine, would be appearing outside of mainland Europe for only the second time, had a mediocre record, having picked up nine defeats over a twenty-five-contest career. It was supposed to be a straightforward workout for Caldwell, as the prospect of his rematch with Gilroy loomed. It turned out, however, to be a bad night for him.

A cut erupted over Caldwell's right eye after a clash of heads in the fifth round. The *Irish Times* labelled it a 'flagrant butt' by Atlan, who, it added, 'had used his head as an extra fist throughout the fight'. It was an injury to the same eye which had forced Caldwell to retire against Gilroy. Despite being well ahead, he was again at the mercy of the ringside doctor. At the beginning of the sixth round, the referee indicated to Caldwell that he had just three minutes to stop the Frenchman. Atlan evaded Caldwell and held on for dear life; the medic was called, and Caldwell was ordered to retire.

It was a devastating result, caused by the reopening of a wound which had not been given sufficient time to heal. Immediately, the rematch with Gilroy was called into question. Docherty claimed that the arctic weather had affected Caldwell's ability to train, and that he was, therefore, not at his best. Tellingly, Docherty revealed that Caldwell had refused to enter a new agreement with him, leaving him potentially a free agent. The feud between manager and boxer remained as bitter as ever. Rumours of a final split persisted.

Freddie Gilroy was scheduled to fight his old foe Johnny Morrisey on 21 March at Glasgow's Kelvin Hall, in a non-title bout set at nine stone, promoted by Solomons. He was expected to prevail yet again against Morrisey, who had been stopped in January by Howard Winstone in a clash for the British featherweight crown. Solomons indicated that once Gilroy had come through his warm-up fights, a date would be set for the keenly anticipated rematch of the two Belfast heroes. That was the plan.

Disappointment, however, was to strike for Gilroy three weeks prior to his date with Morrisey, when his nose was broken while he was sparring with fellow Belfast professional Peter Lavery at the St John Bosco gym. Early in the year, Gilroy had undergone a minor procedure to address constant nosebleeds he had been having since the Caldwell fight. Now doctors warned that he could be facing permanent damage; he was forced to withdraw from his fight in Glasgow.

Caldwell's defeat in February, coupled with Gilroy's injury, put paid to Solomons's plans to host a rematch in the King's Hall in April 1963. With the Gilroy camp holding out for at least one warm-up fight prior to meeting Caldwell, the prospect of the fight taking place even before the autumn was diminishing by the day. Rumour is the lifeblood of boxing, and soon the media began to question whether Gilroy or Caldwell would ever box again.

In May, Gilroy, suffering from weight problems, voluntarily relinquished his position as number-one challenger to Rollo's European title, clearing the way for Caldwell to have a crack at the Italian. By June, it was reported that Gilroy had not trained in three months and that his weight had gone up to over twelve stone. In the *Irish Times*, Terry Leigh-Lye reported that he had visited Belfast that month, where one wag had told him – with great exaggeration, based on local gossip, no doubt – that, 'Wee Freddie has £30,000 in the bank and the boy is no longer interested in fighting.' Within weeks, John Bromley in the *Daily Mirror* was reporting that Gilroy had turned down a £1,000 offer to fight George Bowes for a second time. Bowes was ranked as the chief challenger to Gilroy, but McAree's silence was deafening, which added to the speculation.

The battle of words and constants rumours concerning both boxers persisted over the summer months. Then, on the morning of 11 September, Gilroy got the all-clear from his doctor regarding his nose injury, and it was announced that he intended to return to the ring within six weeks. It was the news that his loyal fans had been praying for daily. The stipulation, however, was that Gilroy would be allowed a warm-up contest at 9st 3lb before he met Caldwell. According to Jimmy McAree, 'Freddie has accumulated a lot of weight and needs time to work that excess off gradually.'

This idea, however, was thrown out within days by the British Boxing Board. It was losing patience, and ruled that Gilroy had been permitted too much time to get himself fit, and that his procrastinating was impacting on the prospects of other boxers, especially Caldwell. He was ordered to fight Caldwell by the end of October. The Board's secretary, Teddy Waltham, conveyed the verdict to McAree, and Gilroy was so incensed that he was reported to have threatened retirement. McAree was furious, claiming that his boxer was being treated unfairly. 'There is no way that Freddie will be down to 8st 6lb by the end of next month. He has only received a medical certificate from his specialist giving him clearance to begin sparring in ten days' time,' McAree advised the press.

A week later, both Gilroy and Caldwell were upstaged in Belfast by the visit of the world heavyweight champion, Sonny Liston, as part of his touring exhibition. Prominent in the media scrum which accompanied Liston was Gilroy, who posed for pictures with the heavyweight in Belfast's North Street. It was apparent that the exile Gilroy had endured in the previous months was over, as he looked happy, despite carrying some excess poundage.

Thousands craned their necks to see the world champion, whose appearance in Belfast had been secured by the joint promotion team of Belfast's George Connell and Glasgow's Peter Keenan. Keenan was a wealthy man and, since his retirement after his defeat to Gilroy in 1959, had reinvented himself as a promoter. He had masterminded the visit of Liston to the British Isles but, more importantly, he had entered into an agreement with Connell which gave the men the exclusive right to promote in Belfast's Ulster Hall and King's Hall.

As for Sonny Liston, who was fresh from knocking out Floyd Patterson for the second time, his visit to Belfast was a procession of staged photographs adorned with shillelaghs and laced with blarney. Margaret Jameson, a twenty-one-year-old Belfast store model, was sacked by her employer for taking time out of the office to catch a glimpse of Liston at a function in a rival shop. Unluckily for Miss Jameson, she was pictured in that evening's *Belfast Telegraph* planting a kiss on Liston's cheek. 'I wondered what he looked like,'

Jameson explained. 'He looks so tough in his photographs, so I just went along with the request from the cameraman to kiss him.'

When her boss, George Major, saw her picture in the paper, he sacked her on the spot and declared, 'If all our staff visited rival stores during working hours, where would we be?' The following evening, Saturday, 21 September, the crowd at the Ulster Hall was left somewhat short-changed by what they saw of the world champion. He entered the ring to great applause, performed a bit of skipping to his theme tune, 'Night Train', sparred a couple of rounds and then left. The crowd was less than impressed, but at least boxing in Belfast was back on the agenda.

With the clock ticking, it took a pleading letter from Gilroy's doctor to force the British Boxing Board to back away from its demand that he defend the title in late October. It granted him an extension, but only of four weeks – and with the proviso that neither he nor Caldwell be allowed warm-up bouts. *Boxing News*, the trade paper of the British fight industry, was fully behind the Board's decision, pointing out that Gilroy had been inactive for almost a full year, and it was patently unfair on those boxers aspiring to secure his Lonsdale Belt.

McAree was incensed at the turn of events. 'Even though we offered to surrender the titles should Gilroy be injured in a warm-up fight, the Board was not impressed,' he told the *Irish News*. In frustration, he accused the Board of acting like 'dictators'. Not surprisingly, Caldwell expressed his satisfaction at the decision; the Cold-Eyed Killer had not disguised his frustration at the on-off nature of the rematch, and the animosity between the boxers was palpable. The bottom line was that neither boxer was earning money in the ring, and Caldwell's frustration was well-founded in light of Gilroy's inability to agree a date for the fight.

It was now very apparent that Gilroy was struggling to make the weight. However, that fact was overshadowed by the fall-out between Peter Keenan and Jack Solomons over the right to stage the fight at the King's Hall. Keenan was blocking Solomons from using the King's Hall for the rematch. (Connell wanted to break his agreement with Keenan and promote the fight with Solomons.) A last-gasp attempt to broker a deal occurred in Belfast on Sunday, 3 November. It was a powerful gathering of managers and boxers which saw Solomons fly in from London to try and negotiate an agreement.

Keenan stood defiant, insisting that he, in partnership with Connell, held the exclusive right to promote in the King's Hall. As such, Solomons would have to compensate Keenan substantially to step aside. Jolly Jack was a gambling man, and he was betting on the power of Belfast public opinion to pressure Keenan into capitulating. Keenan, however, knew how much the fight was worth and was not for moving. After five hours of talks in the Grand Central Hotel in Belfast, the talks broke up without agreement.

John Caldwell spoke to the media at the hotel for a press conference at the conclusion of the unresolved negotiations. He underlined his view that Belfast was the only place the fight should take place. 'I have not boxed for ten months. I need the money for this fight,' said Caldwell. 'Like Freddie Gilroy, I am a Belfast man and this fight belongs to Belfast, but I must fight even if is in Timbuktu or in London.' It was obvious that the pressure to seal a deal was at crisis point.

Freddie Gilroy was not at the press conference, but Jimmy McAree was. 'What makes me annoyed is that Gilroy has been thrown into the battle of the promoters like a lamb to the slaughter; all they do is bicker, and Freddie is not considered at all,' McAree said. He knew that the bottom line for Connell, Keenan and Solomons was making lots of money off the backs of the two boxers; Caldwell and Gilroy were mere cash cows in a nasty squabble among the moneymen. With the on-off nature of the rematch with Gilroy, Caldwell had turned down some lucrative fight offers. The Cold-Eyed Killer had lost out on many thousands of pounds waiting on Gilroy, and the delay was hurting the family man in his pocket.

Solomons left for London in foul form, giving Keenan twenty-four hours to make a decision. Alas, there was to be no meeting of minds and Solomons, as the contract-holder, played the nuclear option by adding the rematch to his bill in London on 26 November. While claiming to be upset that the fight was going to London, Solomons assured the media that, 'if either of the boys show good enough form to justify a match with Éder Jofre, I would arrange a fight at Wembley within three months'. As a sop to those Belfast fans that would have to travel to London to see their heroes, Solomons promised to reserve a block of the 'cheaper seats' at Wembley. The fight that had 'belonged to Belfast', according to Solomons, was now headed to London. There were to be further twists, though.

On 7 November, the rumours about Gilroy's inability to make the weight for the Caldwell rematch were proved true when McAree announced that his fighter was to relinquish his titles and forego the contest. The news broke after McAree had sent a telegram to the British Boxing Board, saying that Gilroy had 'health reasons' for dropping out. Gilroy had walked away from the prospect of collecting the lion's share of a £6,000 purse. 'Why this announcement now? Why? Why?' thundered Solomons to Sydney Hulls of the *Daily Express*. The boxing world was stunned. Solomons immediately moved to cancel the bill, which was to have been headlined by a clash between Henry Cooper and the American Jefferson Davis. All that remained for him now was to apportion blame and to seek redress through the British Boxing Board for the losses he had incurred. Gilroy and McAree were in trouble.

The Press Association was somewhat facetious in its reporting of Gilroy's abdication. 'An over-indulgence in fish and chips and ice cream has cost Freddie Gilroy his British and Empire bantamweight boxing titles', it reported. The *Daily Express* referred to Gilroy's 'calamitous and calorific taste in fish and chips' as the reason why he had lost the fight against the scales. Gilroy had weighed ten and a half stone in September, but, after losing sixteen pounds, he was still almost a stone over the agreed fighting weight. 'Boiling off' the remaining weight would, according to McAree, 'be almost certainly injurious to the boy's health.'

McAree blamed Solomons for the situation, claiming that the promoter knew Gilroy had weight problems and had promised that, if he had secured the right to co-promote the fight with Connell at the King's Hall, he would have made a request to have it postponed to allow Gilroy to shed the excess weight. Despite the mess, retirement was not on the Gilroy agenda. He announced that he would have his first fight as a featherweight in the New Year. This, however, was never to be.

Inevitably, with Solomons's bill at Wembley Arena now cancelled, the false camaraderie among the boxers, managers and promoters disintegrated into bitterness. The question of who would pay for the fiasco remained unresolved. The British Boxing Board would decide who was to blame for the breaching of the contract, and things looked bleak for Gilroy and McAree as Solomons pressed for compensation. Solomons was claiming a cool £5,000, but had indicated that he would settle for £3,000. As the world stopped to witness the burial of John Fitzgerald Kennedy, the petty squabble regarding the compensation for the cancelled Wembley show was played out in front of the boxing officials.

After a lengthy meeting, the Board, predictably, found in favour of Solomons, and imposed £2,000 in damages on Gilroy and McAree. The two Belfast men, who were represented by the Belfast solicitor John Turner, were ordered to pay the money within six months. It was a painful outcome, despite upbeat talk of an appeal. It could have been worse for Gilroy and McAree, though. There was a painful lesson also for Belfast promoter George Connell at the hearing, when Solomons was awarded a nominal £100 in damages (and £300 in expenses) for Connell's failure to honour their 'gentleman's agreement' to stage the rematch in Belfast. This agreement was a verbal contract made in the King's Hall ring at the end of the Gilroy-Caldwell encounter. Solomons was not a man to be crossed, according to the British Boxing Board.

The press's commentary on the fiasco was scathing. Gilroy and Solomons shouldered most of the blame, but Peter Keenan got his share too. Jim Davey, in the *Irish Press*, wrote that professional boxing in Ireland was on its knees as a result of the fall-out. Writing in rather exaggerated prose, Davey stated, 'I am not crying for Freddie Gilroy; far from it. I am crying for professional boxing in this country. I don't know what can save it now.' The article continued in the same somewhat peculiar vein when he added that big-time boxing in Belfast was 'now in the last couple of seconds of the last round, glassy-eyed as a China doll on the mantelpiece, just waiting for the final count to rise from eight, nine – OUT.' Davey ended with a puerile flourish, stating that the Belfast public had lost faith in professional boxing and predicting that the next promotion in the city would not 'draw enough members of the public to crush a bunch of grapes'.

20.

'YOU USED TO BE A CONTENDER, DIDN'T YOU?'

With Freddie Gilroy now just a fading and sour memory, John Caldwell began to pick up the pieces of his own boxing career. The British Boxing Board acted almost immediately, matching Caldwell with George Bowes for Gilroy's vacant titles – a fight that would be promoted by Solomons.

Just before Christmas 1963, a feature on Caldwell was published in the *Irish Independent*. Journalist Tom Keogh visited the comfortable Caldwell home on the outskirts of west Belfast. There, Keogh found little evidence of Caldwell the fighter, discovering instead a doting father and loyal husband, who chatted amicably as he nursed his four-year-old son, John, who had just returned from hospital after having had his tonsils removed. With his two-year-old daughter Patricia hanging round his neck, Caldwell spoke of his pride in having worn the green of Ireland.

Relaxed and sipping tea in a home which, Keogh noted, was

strangely lacking in boxing memorabilia, Caldwell also talked about the pressure to earn money as a fighter and the heartbreak of having to leave his children to train in Glasgow. After this quiet Christmas spent at home, Caldwell returned to Scotland to train for the fight with Bowes for the British and Empire bantamweight titles. The loneliness and homesickness began again in earnest.

With the King's Hall out of bounds for Solomons, the promoter had hired Belfast's 2,800-capacity Ritz Cinema in Great Victoria Street for the Caldwell-Bowes clash on 20 January. Luck, however, deserted Solomons when a telegram arrived from the Bowes camp, telling him that the fight was off because Bowes had sustained a leg injury. Undeterred, the promoter secured the services of Belgian champion Jean Renard as a late substitute for Caldwell.

Solomons – rather presumptuously – offered the winner of the Caldwell-Renard clash a fight with Gilroy. He believed Gilroy's retirement was mere bluff and, despite the fact that he had been the prime mover in having Gilroy and McAree fined in November, both boxer and trainer would come begging to him as their money dried up. Regardless, the Caldwell-Renard match fell through when the Belgian withdrew four days before the fight because of a disagreement over money. Solomons cancelled the show but re-booked the Ritz for 5 March, giving Bowes a full six weeks to recover before the title fight. Caldwell's frustration at the whole escapade was plain for all to see.

To say that John Caldwell was a complicated individual is an understatement. Shy, outwardly cold, independent and, at times, utterly stubborn, he was dismayed by the professional fight business and had lost any enjoyment that the sport had previously provided him with. Speaking to the *Belfast Telegraph* in late-February, he was forthright in his views on boxing. On fans, he announced, 'They're parasites, all parasites.' On his critics, 'They're cowboys; if there were no actors, there would be no critics.' And, on boxing itself, he told

Jack Magowan, 'I'm only in the game for money. I used to love fighting, but not any more. Still, it's the only job I know.'

These were the words of a truly unhappy man, who was facing up to the reality of a waning career. He had crossed his own personal Rubicon, and boxing had become a painful chore, a game he had fallen out of love with. Magowan labelled Caldwell an enigma and a 'problem child'. But, given all that Caldwell had endured during 1962 and 1963, who could blame him for being angry? Solomons held the contract for the Bowes fight, while Caldwell's manager-in-name-only, Sam Docherty, with whom the boxer rarely spoke, pulled the strings in the background. For Caldwell, there was no alternative. His heart, though, was anywhere but in boxing.

By Thursday, 5 March, the Ritz, a tired, gaudy, dust-encrusted art-deco palace, which had famously played host to The Beatles four months previously, was ready for Caldwell's return. A ring had been erected in the orchestra pit. For Caldwell, it was a sort of homecoming; the cinema was five hundred yards from his former Cyprus Street home. Bowes, who had famously had his ankle shattered by the reverberating power of a Freddie Gilroy punch in 1958, had won his crack at the title the hard way. At twenty-seven, his time was running out, but a run of six wins in 1963 had landed him his place in the ring that night. Tickets for the fight sold out quickly, as Belfast seemed to take Caldwell back into its heart. For the winner, there was the prospect of a fight against European champion Risto Luukkonen.

Referee Ike Powell reminded the boxers of the Queensberry Rules, and the two men stood ready under the dazzling spotlights. A massive roar in support of Caldwell emanated throughout the arena. In the second round, Caldwell had blood streaming from Bowes's nose, courtesy of an all-action style of combination punching. Despite showing a degree of ring-rustiness, Caldwell peppered Bowes's face with lefts and rights, which had the former Durham miner in trouble throughout the fourth and fifth rounds. By the seventh, Bowes's left eye was flowing like a red river, and the referee wisely called a halt to the fight – much to the delight of the home crowd, and the apparent dismay of Bowes. Later, Bowes would claim that Caldwell had caught him with his head, but the fact remained that he had been well out-boxed. In the ring, Caldwell, with his son John displayed proudly in his arms, was presented again with a Lonsdale Belt; the famine was over, and Belfast had a new ban-tamweight champion of Britain.

Jack Solomons was busy telling the media that he had incurred a £1,000 loss by hosting the fight in Belfast. Still, he immediately began to make plans for Caldwell to defend his crown against either Walter Magowan or Howard Winstone, with the winner meeting the 'retired' Freddie Gilroy. In the background, Solomons was also nego-tiating with Éder Jofre to promote the Brazilian on a tour of Britain, the highlight of which would be a defence of his title against Caldwell. That, though, was merely a pipe dream; a return fight with the Belfast boxer was never going to happen.

In April 1964, Caldwell's comeback plans were hampered when the British Boxing Board severed its links with the European Boxing Union. Caldwell had been scheduled to fight French-Tunisian Felix Brami in an eliminator for Risto Luukkonen's European title on 14 April, but a fall-out between the British and European boxing bodies put that contest on hold. The sacking of Edouard Rabret as EBU presi-dent, as part of an internal power struggle, prompted the British Board to withdraw in protest. Caldwell's plans to fight Luukkonen for the con-tinental title were effectively shelved. With no fight in the offing, a fur-ther bust-up involving Caldwell and Docherty was now inevitable.

The mutual loathing that existed between Caldwell and Docherty festered throughout the spring of 1964, as the lay-off ate into Caldwell's diminishing savings. Their final breakup would occur in – of all places – Accra, the capital of Ghana. The occasion was the 9 May clash between Floyd Robertson and Sugar Ramos for the world featherweight title, a bill Solomons was promoting. Robertson had won the Commonwealth featherweight crown at the King's Hall in 1960, when he defeated Percy Lewis. During the three years Robertson had spent in Belfast, the local fighting public had taken the Ghanaian into their hearts. Crucially, Robertson was a stable-mate of Caldwell's, managed by Docherty.

With John at a loose end in Belfast, and the Ghanaian government funding the promotion to the tune of £35,000, Solomons and Docherty agreed to add Caldwell's name to the bill. The plan was that Caldwell would box an exhibition against a local opponent as a warm-up to the main event. However, if Brazil had been a strange experience for Caldwell in 1962, Ghana put him into serious culture shock. Grinding poverty, hissing cockroaches, blinding sun and stomach trouble all soon took their toll on the Falls Road man.

On the fourth day of the trip, Caldwell, missing his family, fed up, and suffering from dysentery, sunstroke and mild malaria, packed his bags, left his hotel and boarded a flight back to London. Docherty and Solomons were incandescent with rage. For Docherty, it had been a double snub, as Caldwell had again refused to sign a new con-tract that would tie him to the Glasgow bookmaker until 1967. Jolly Jack was spitting fire over the abrupt departure, telling the press that Caldwell had 'not heard the end of this; I will reclaim every penny of what it cost to bring him here'.

In Accra, Robertson would lose to Ramos in a split decision before forty thousand fans, leaving Docherty and Solomons disap-pointed, but decidedly richer. After the fight, Solomons began a cru-sade to extract his pound of flesh from Caldwell. However, any notion that Caldwell would repay Solomons an estimated £1,000 for his failure to box in Ghana was scuppered when it was discovered that no contract had existed. A telegram from Solomons inviting Caldwell to Ghana as a guest was naturally not considered to be a binding agreement.

Solomons wrote to the British Boxing Board to demand that Caldwell be disciplined, claiming the boxer 'owed' him a fight. Solomons's plea was ignored, though, since that was really a matter for the boxer and the promoter to resolve. By now, Docherty and Caldwell had parted very acrimoniously; monies Docherty owed to Caldwell remained unpaid and would become the subject of an unsuccessful court case in 1967. Caldwell accepted an offer to come under the wing of London promoter Burt McCarthy, who, along with trainer Tony Mancini, seemed determined to oversee a change of luck for the Irishman. Their first move was to match Caldwell against former Spanish bantamweight champion Rafael Fernandez, at the World Sporting Club in Mayfair on 5 October.

In late September, Caldwell upped sticks from his training camp in London and returned to Belfast, citing 'family problems'. McCarthy, though, was confident that Caldwell would return in time to fight Fernandez. 'I have three fights lined up for Ireland's "forgotten champion". There is no reason why he should not reach the top of Everest again,' McCarthy said. The London manager was preparing Caldwell in the long term for a defence of his British bantamweight crown against the up-and-coming Alan Rudkin, a Liverpudlian who had won seventeen of his previous eighteen bouts. That contest would be the big-money fight that both McCarthy and Caldwell craved, but Fernandez stood in the way. The day before the date with Fernandez, Caldwell dutifully returned to London and McCarthy breathed a sigh of relief. That month, Caldwell was named number thirty-nine in the world bantamweight rankings; it was going to require a tremendous effort to climb back into world contention.

In a haze of expensive cigar smoke, under the finest of chandeliers, John Caldwell entered the ring to polite applause from the tuxedo-clad audience in the World Sporting Club. Having already polished off an expensive meal, the well-to-do patrons were enjoying fine wines and brandies as the entertainment began. Boxing matches in the World Sporting Club were merely incidental distractions for the audience, who saw the evening as an opportunity to mix with their own kind and talk business. Regardless, the man from the Falls Road in Belfast gave a display which dispelled any notion that he was on the verge of retirement.

Caldwell peppered Fernandez with neat left hooks, which prompted well-mannered appreciation and encouragement from the patrons. The Spaniard was a brave fighter who refused to yield in the face of the onslaught. However, the end came in the eighth round, with blood flowing from Fernandez's eye, when referee Pat Floyd stopped the contest. It had been a most impressive display by Caldwell, who had sent out a clear message that he was – at twenty-six – a fighter still to be feared in British and European boxing terms.

The next appointment for Caldwell, scheduled for 11 November, was a Peter Keenan-promoted bill at the Paisley Ice Rink. His opponent, Jackie Brown, had been knocked out by Gilroy at the same arena in 1961, but Brown had gone on to excel as a flyweight, taking the British and Empire titles – which he then lost to Walter Magowan in May 1963. On moving up to bantamweight, Brown had won the Scottish Area Title by beating Tommy Burgoyne in February 1964. He was not expected, however, to cause Caldwell any serious problems.

Caldwell travelled reluctantly to Glasgow to prepare again under Joe Aitcheson; he was supremely fit ahead of the contest. The fight, however, saw Caldwell at his worst. As it progressed, it became evident that Caldwell would need a knockout to win. The last round, though, saw Brown dominate and, at the bell, Aitcheson quite noticeably prevented Caldwell from crossing the ring to congratulate Brown. Referee Ian MacFadyen studied his card laboriously before calling the contest a draw. It was a decision that drew a crescendo of boos from a crowd convinced Brown had won easily. Caldwell was nowhere near the boxer he had been three years previously. The end of a glittering career was coming into view.

In mid-November, the British Boxing Board nominated Alan Rudkin as the mandatory challenger for Caldwell's title. Rudkin stood on the crest of a wave, having been voted boxer of the year by the British Boxing Writers' Club. Many deemed Caldwell's hold on the bantamweight title tenuous. On 25 November, though, Caldwell appeared again in front of a tuxedo-clad audience, this time at the plush Hilton Hotel in London's Park Lane. Rudkin's manager, Bobby Neill, was a keen observer as John faced the Nigerian Orizu Obilaso. Caldwell redeemed himself somewhat, with an assured victory on points.

In the opening minute, Caldwell caught the Obilaso with a tremendous right hand to the chin, but the Nigerian refused to go down, and the fight went the distance. Caldwell was cautioned twice for holding and took some punishment in the last round, but he held out for an easy victory. Within days, Caldwell's defence of his bantamweight crown against Rudkin was agreed for Nottingham Ice Rink on 22 March 1965. With the King's Hall out of commission, Belfast's fight fans would be robbed of an opportunity to see Caldwell box. Would John Caldwell ever fight in Belfast again?

Alan Rudkin hailed from Liverpool, which, at that time, was the centre of the music world. At twenty-two, he represented a new generation of boxers which was coming to the fore in the 'swinging' 1960s. Caldwell seemed ripe for the taking. This defence of his title was literally 'make or break' for his boxing career. A defeat to Rudkin would relegate him to the 'has-beens' class, while a win could prove to be a lucrative change of luck. With only seven fights in three years, Caldwell had suffered through injury and managerial disputes; his long periods of inactivity could easily be exposed by Rudkin, a boxer who had enjoyed tremendous form throughout 1964.

Three weeks of all-out training in Glasgow saw Caldwell fighting fit as early March arrived. However, the bookmakers made the Belfast fighter a complete outsider to retain his crown. The Monday-night meeting of the boxers drew a capacity crowd to the arena, the vast majority of whom were shouting for Rudkin. The fight began cautiously, with Caldwell adopting his familiar style and throwing punches with ease. The third round, though, was a disaster for Caldwell. A Rudkin punch cracked John's nose and caused internal bleeding, which had him literally choking on his own blood.

From then on, it was damage limitation for Caldwell, who fought on bravely until the referee halted proceedings in the tenth round. Regardless, Rudkin had effectively out-boxed a tiring Caldwell and was the new and worthy champion. The Lonsdale Belt was now around the waist of a new titleholder, who would go on to prove his greatness by challenging for the WBC title on three separate occasions. In 1972, Rudkin's last fight as a professional saw him beat Johnny Clarke to claim the British and Commonwealth bantamweight titles. He was found dead on a street in Liverpool in September 2010. He was sixty-eight.

Caldwell was now a man whose glittering past was confined to the history books. Of immediate concern, though, was the damage to his nose, which required surgery. John's breathing had been affected badly by the injury, and the specialists in Belfast's Royal Victoria Hospital ordered him to take at least six months out of the ring. Manager Burt McCarthy was adamant that the injury should be allowed to heal. 'The boy can't go on like this,' said McCarthy. 'Either this nose trouble is cleared up for good, or I will urge him to give up. I'm not going to allow any boxer of mine to risk his health in this way.' In addition to his nose injury, Caldwell was a changed man: he lacked the urgency and hunger which had brought him to the cusp of becoming the undisputed world champion in Brazil in 1962.

John Caldwell was to have one more outing. With his nose injury receiving the all-clear in mid-September, he was matched on 12 October against Monty Laud in Brighton's Hotel Metropole. Laud, from St Ives in Cambridgeshire, had enjoyed a fine amateur career, having won the ABA flyweight title in 1963. At merely twenty-one, he had won eight and drawn three of his eleven contests and was seen as an up-and-coming champion, who would be too fast and eager for Caldwell. Any notion that Caldwell would get a chance to meet Rudkin in a rematch was scuppered by his manager, Bobby Neil, who said, 'Sure, we'll give Caldwell a chance at revenge, but there are bigger fish to fry and domestic matters can wait.' The 'bigger fish' was world champion Masahiko 'Fighting' Harada, whom Rudkin was scheduled to fight in Japan in November.

The reality was that Caldwell was bordering on journeyman status. The big fights, the massive crowds and the glory were mere memories as he climbed through the ropes for the last time, in front of a decidedly indifferent Brighton crowd. The fight went Laud's way from the beginning. The *Glasgow Herald*'s boxing correspondent commented that 'Caldwell lacked speed and a lot of the old fire. Where he used to put his punches together, they came one at a time, and the destructive element which took him to the top was strangely lacking.'

Laud soon realised that he was not facing the Caldwell of old and, with speed and the ambition of youth, he scored with ease to win decisively. Caldwell returned to Belfast and hung up his gloves. For a man who had lit up Irish, British, European and world boxing, it was a sad ending to a brilliant but unfulfilled career. It was back to the mediocre world of trade, tools, tedious jobs and a weekly pay packet. John Caldwell, like Freddie Gilroy, was yesterday's man, in boxing terms.

21.

A DIMINISHING LEGACY

At merely twenty-eight years of age, Freddie Gilroy had seemingly slammed the door on his boxing career. The fine levied on him and Jimmy McAree remained unpaid on principle, and the British Boxing Board stripped both men of their boxing licences permanently. Gilroy, however, was thinking of the future. He invested his estimated £30,000 in earnings in the licensing trade and took possession of the Tivoli Bar in Manor Street, in the coastal town of Donaghadee, eighteen miles from Belfast. Gilroy's bar enjoyed a brisk trade, and he was soon showing his class as captain of the bar's darts team in the local leagues. Despite his public adamance that he would never again enter the ring, the rumours persisted that Ireland's most popular boxer would consider a comeback.

Boxing in Belfast was going through a bad patch. The King's Hall had not hosted a bill since the epic clash of Gilroy and Caldwell in 1962. For local promoter George Connell, times were lean. Without a star with the class of Gilroy, the Belfast public was largely apathetic. John Caldwell's attempted resurgence had been met with indifference; Gilroy was the man the Belfast public wanted to see again. In

October 1964, rumours surfaced that Solomons and Connell had resolved their differences and were seeking Gilroy to top a bill at the King's Hall in early 1965, fighting as a featherweight. Freddie, it seemed, was keen to bolster talk of a comeback. 'Once a fighter, always a fighter,' he told Jack Magowan in the *Belfast Telegraph*. 'Anyone who loves the game as much as I do never loses the urge to fight.'

Weighing in at almost eleven stone, Gilroy said he would be returning to the gym to commence training, with a view to making the featherweight limit by January 1965. 'If I can't get down to that weight – and nothing beats a darned good try – then I'll hang up my gloves for good,' he told Magowan. However, the fact that Gilroy had had his licence revoked by the British Boxing Board remained the biggest impediment to his comeback. In London, Solomons was insistent that he be paid his due in full before the Belfast man would be allowed to re-apply for his licence. Gilroy and McAree were adamant that they would not pay their fine.

In the background, a young promoter had entered the scene in Belfast who was also keen to get Gilroy back into the ring. Tyrone-born bookmaker Barney Eastwood had made his fortune with a string of betting shops and had big plans to reinvigorate the sport in Ireland. However, in the face of Gilroy's insistence that he would not return without McAree as his manager, and the deadlock with Solomons, this effort fizzled. Boxing in Belfast did enjoy a small renaissance under Eastwood, and the Ulster Hall hosted some attractive bills. However, without the class of a Gilroy or a Caldwell, the fight game petered out in the city, as Northern Ireland headed into its own abyss in 1969. The King's Hall would not host a boxing bill from the epic Caldwell vs. Gilroy clash of 1962 until Hugh Russell defended his British bantamweight title against Davy Larmour at the venue in March 1983.

While Gilroy continued to raise a family and play the genial host in the Tivoli Bar, political tensions on the street began to put his ownership of the bar on borrowed time. With the onslaught of the Troubles, the fact that Gilroy, a Catholic from Ardoyne, pursued his business interests in the Loyalist Donaghadee made him an easy target. Soon, the hate-mail flooded into the bar and threats arrived on a daily basis by phone and by post. Being a sports star who had crossed the religious divide meant nothing in a society where sectarian hatred had bubbled up again. One morning, Freddie arrived to open his bar, only to find a red cross painted on the door. The men of violence eventually struck the Tivoli Bar on 27 February 1972, with a gelignite bomb that destroyed the premises. 'That bomb attack destroyed me inside,' recalled Gilroy.

> I had a great relationship with the people of Donaghadee and now my life was in tatters. I stood in the wreckage the next morning and swore that I would leave Ireland, as there seemed to be no future for my family and me. I was in despair. Everything I had in my life had been devastated . . . I had to sell the bar for a rock-bottom price. It was soul-destroying.

The only casualty in the bomb attack on the bar was the resident parrot, Joey. Some less-than-scrupulous patrons of the bar had taught the bird to say disparaging things about the Pope. Irony was always an integral part of Northern Ireland's conflict.

With boxing in Northern Ireland enduring its own crisis, a return to the game he loved was no option for Gilroy. In October 1972, Freddie and Kay emigrated to Australia with their children, Laura, Kim, Paula and Freddie junior. In Belfast, almost five hundred people lost their lives as a result of the Troubles in 1972. Gilroy's patch of north Belfast was at the epicentre of the hatred. The Gilroy family put down its roots in Blacktown, outside Sydney. Freddie made a living as the manager of the local working men's club. The family were comfortable and happy, but homesickness for Belfast was taking hold.

With Freddie in Australia, first his mother and then his father passed away. These were sickening blows for the former boxer. When Kay's mother became ill in early 1977, the family decided to return to Ireland. They tried to settle in Dublin but, with Gilroy's savings dwindling, life was tough in the capital. Within a year, he and his family found themselves back in Belfast. With his fortune now gone, and working at the Fortwilliam Golf Club, Freddie entered into dark times which lasted for almost a decade.

The bottle began to take control. 'There was just something going on in my head – an awful, unhappy feeling – be it from quitting fighting or being bombed out of my pub,' he said. Gilroy could not cope. He wanted oblivion. He lost almost everything. 'The years between 1978 and 1988 were ten empty years. I couldn't help myself and turned to the booze for comfort,' he recalled. With alcoholism taking grip, Gilroy's marriage broke up and he found himself living with his brother Teddy in Ardoyne's Northwick Drive.

In January 1986, Gilroy's prized Lonsdale Belt, which had been valued at £24,000 in 1984, went missing. The belt had been Freddie's pride and joy, the only trophy he had retained from a glittering professional career. He maintained that he had loaned the belt to his former employer and friend Frankie Bannon, and that the belt was still in Bannon's possession. Friends of Bannon, however, refuted the allegation and claimed that Gilroy had left the belt on a bus while drunk – which was taken as an insult by Gilroy. The belt has never been recovered, which still hurts Gilroy immensely.

> Not a day goes by without somebody asking about my belt, and I just fob them off. If I kept thinking about it all the time it would destroy me . . . Then there's the embarrassment factor, too. All these stories about me leaving it on a bus when I was drunk are simply not true.

Freddie Gilroy's recovery began when he met his second wife, Bernadette, a woman he refers to as his saviour. He went to counselling for his drink problem and has been sober ever since. He again became a well-known face in Belfast city centre, as a car-parking attendant, but most of the customers had no idea of the illustrious career of the man who handed them their change.

John Caldwell's flirtation with alcohol was long and, ultimately, devastating. On retirement, boxing was erased totally from his life; his skills and experience were not handed on to the budding pugilists of Andersonstown. His bitterness about the sport was caused by the treatment he had received at the hands of Sam Docherty. In 1967, Caldwell sued Docherty for the money he believed was outstanding from his career. In the Glasgow Sheriff Court, without receipts or contract, Caldwell's case was thrown out.

He remained a celebrity in his hometown, although, given his modest nature, many locals were never to realise just how famous he had once been. He returned to the plumbing trade and, in the 1970s, he and his family moved briefly to Canada. Work was hard to find, though, and the pangs of homesickness soon brought the Caldwells back to Belfast. His marriage ended as the drink took hold, and the battle against alcoholism was lost. He became a pitiful, lonely figure in the bars of Andersonstown, accompanied by the ever-present pint of Guinness. People learned to leave him to his own company, and he kept his thoughts to himself.

By the early 1990s, Caldwell had been placed in sheltered accommodation in Andersonstown, and he walked each morning to his daughter Patricia's house before spending his days in the local hostelries. His greatest opponent, cancer, soon landed a devastating blow. An operation to his throat patched up the damage, but he was a pitiful sight. He fought the cancer with all the courage and tough-minded resolve he once showed in the ring. Life, he knew, had dealt him a foul blow, but he was still smiling.

In October 2002, Belfast Lord Mayor Alex Maskey held a reception in the city hall to commemorate the fortieth anniversary of the Caldwell-Gilroy encounter. It was a night of sheer nostalgia, with the boxers taking centre stage. In the ornate Lord Mayor's Parlour, Caldwell looked decidedly ill. 'The toast is to two proud and gallant warriors from another era,' said Maskey, welcoming close to 150 friends of boxing, many of whom were former champions. Fans came from London, Dublin and Cork to watch a thirty-minute video of the fight. It was a snapshot of a period of glory that had been condemned to the sidelines of history.

Caldwell lost his battle with cancer on Friday, 10 July 2009, surrounded by his family. His funeral in Belfast saw a gathering of the great and the good of Irish boxing. Freddie Gilroy was not in attendance, as he was holidaying in west Cork. Freddie's absence was noted by the media. Mourners were told that he had Caldwell had 'fought the good fight'. His glory days were fondly remembered by Harry Perry, Jim McCourt and Hugh Russell, who gathered at St Agnes's Church.

As his funeral cortège made its way along the Falls Road, his grandchildren carried his boxing gloves, his Olympic towel, a trophy and a framed picture of him in action. Several floral wreaths adorned the hearse, including one shaped like a boxing ring, which read 'Our Dad, boxing legend'. His burial took place just twenty-four hours after his first great-grandchild was born.

Addressing the mourners, Father Peter Owens described John as a 'mild-mannered, quiet and very unassuming' man, who was devoted to his family. 'As a boxer John achieved much, much at which he could legitimately be very proud. But he was proudest of all of his children and grandchildren,' he said.

However, Owens said it was for his boxing achievements that Caldwell would be most remembered. 'John Caldwell is a legend not least in his hometown. He was the greatest fighter that Ireland ever produced. He brought honour to Ireland, to Belfast and the Immaculata club,' he said.

John Caldwell was buried in his Irish Olympic blazer, fifty-three years after he wore it with pride as he received his medal in Australia.